Past-into-Present Series

CLOTHES

Marjorie Wilkerson

Head of History,
Parliament Hill School, Highgate

B. T. BATSFORD LTD   London

First published 1970
© Marjorie Wilkerson, 1970

Filmset by Keyspools Ltd, Golborne, Lancs.

Printed in Great Britain by
Billing & Sons Ltd, Guildford, Surrey
for the Publishers
B. T. BATSFORD LTD, 4 Fitzhardinge Street, London W.1

7134 1766 8

Acknowledgment

The author and publisher would like to thank the following for permission to reproduce the illustrations listed:

Alison Aldburgham and Allen & Unwin Ltd for figs. 42 and 50 from *Shops and Shopping*; Samuel and Mary R. Bancroft Collection, Delaware Art Center for fig. 49; The Bodleian Library for fig. 10; The Trustees of the British Museum for figs. 6, 16 and 31; J. & P. Coats Ltd. for fig. 41; C. W. & P. Cunnington and Michael Joseph Ltd for fig. 28 from *The History of Underclothes*; French Government Tourist Office for fig. 9; Harris Museum and Art Gallery for fig. 40; H. J. Heinz Co. Ltd for fig. 54; Henry E. Huntington Library and Art Gallery for fig. 30; The Illustrated London News for figs. 43 and 48; The Manchester Public Libraries for figs. 18, 20 and 25; The Mansell Collection for figs. 2–5, 11, 12, 14, 21, 22, 37, 39, 55 and 62; Marks and Spencer Ltd for figs. 57 and 58; The Metropolitan Museum of Art for fig. 1; Ministry of Public Buildings and Works for fig. 13; National Film Archive for fig. 53; The Trustees of the National Maritime Museum for fig. 29; The Trustees of the National Portrait Gallery for fig. 63; The Press Association Ltd for fig. 60; Radio Times Hulton Picture Library for figs. 17, 19, 44, 47, 56, 59 and 66; The Trustees of the Tate Gallery for fig. 51; University of Reading for fig. 32; The Trustees of the Victoria and Albert Museum for fig. 15.

Contents

The Illustrations

1 Early Days

Why are the clothes people wore in past times so interesting?

When the archaeologist Schliemann, the poor German boy who had become a millionaire merchant, discovered what he believed to be the golden hoard of the ancient kings of Greece his young Greek wife put on the priceless jewellery. Wearing these adornments, made centuries before Christ was born, it was easy to imagine her as one of the women of ancient Greece.

As we look back at the people who lived in the centuries before ours we imagine them in life, wearing the sort of clothes they would have worn, whether the rough skins of the Stone Age or the swaying crinolines of Victoria's day. What was the style of the day? What was the fashion being worn at the time?

This is a recent idea. Europeans in the Middle Ages knew that the Romans had worn togas. They could see them on the many statues and remains still to be found in Rome. But Tudor actors would still perform a Roman play by Shakespeare wearing a mixture of their own clothes and Roman robes with Eastern details. To their eyes this effect was strange and foreign and, therefore, quite suitable as Roman.

The history of clothing has developed since then. The fashion of any period can be studied in illustrations from the paintings on the walls of tombs, portraits, fashion drawings and, more recently, photographs. What is still not clear from pictures alone is why these particular clothes were worn or when these materials were developed.

Clothes, we presume, are meant to keep people warm. This does not explain why the Ancient Egyptians wore linen, wool and cotton robes in the heat of their climate, whilst in the nineteenth century Charles Darwin found primitive tribes shivering in the chill rain of a cold climate and yet wearing nothing at all.

Clothes have had many uses besides providing warmth. They are worn to make the human body more attractive, to act as a form of decoration, to show what a person does for his living and indicate his place in society. They also reveal something of the wearer's personality. Clothing can provide a uniform, either to make the wearer part of a group (as in the case of a soldier), or to provide a means of standing out alone (as, for example, a king).

The only materials available to the earliest men were the skins and furs that came from the animals they killed for food. But clothes of this kind became stiff and uncomfortable. The leather of skins must be treated to make it softer. Skins could be scraped clean of hair and softened, a process that the American Indians used till recently for the supple tunics they wore under cloaks made of bison skin on which the hair had been left to provide extra warmth. The leather was treated with fats to make it soft, and the Bushmen of Africa still do this today.

By the end of the Old Stone Age women were joining skins together with fish-bone needles and thread of animal sinew or fibres of plants. The flesh was cut from the skins with sharp hand stones; the skin was then stretched out, held down on the ground by pegs, when the remaining flesh and hair was scraped off. The ashes of the fire, fat from animals and some of the liquid from the trees around were used to preserve and soften the skin. Then the skins were worn, still furred on one side for warmth, protection and even camouflage, but softer and cosier on the inside. One garment, therefore, was used where we need two today —an over and an undergarment.

Then it was discovered first how to weave and then how to spin the thread, so that cloth could be made. It was softer, it could be draped and folded, it could be woven into pieces of clothes length. It would need to be worn or sewn in the piece or the rough weaving could unravel. The long piece of cloth would be hung round the body as a shawl, or have a hole cut in the middle for the head, and be pulled together with a belt for the waist. For more leisured occupations the cloth could be simply draped in folds around the body, while children could be swaddled in long lengths of cloth.

These early men were already using the two main styles of clothing which we shall find through history: the loose, simple, draped and folded garment and the more fitted sewn one.

By the New Stone Age man (or woman) had discovered how to spin many short fibres together to make a thread. No-one knows whether it was wool, linen or cotton that was first spun but spindle whorls have been discovered from 10,000 years ago. The earliest woven cloth no longer survives—the threads have rotted away—but the pattern of the cloth remains, pressed on clay. The threads produced by the spindles of the women and, in later days, dyed with the juice of crushed roots and the flowers of plants, were not easy to weave together.

1   Egyptian model of a weaving courtyard.

2 Greek women's clothes, fifth century BC. The women are wearing their festive garments at a feast. Usually men entertained without their womenfolk. Here they wear wreathes in their hair and finely draped cloth.

Weaving is bringing the threads together to make cloth. Darning is a simple form of weaving, and just as the threads set across a hole in darning have to be kept apart as the cross threads are run in and out, so the weaver had to keep his apart when he was making the cloth. At first the long threads we call the 'warp' must have hung down from a piece of wood held high, perhaps between trees. This allowed them to hang straight, each thread weighted by a ball of clay or a stone. The cross threads or 'weft' now had to be run through. To do this more easily every alternate down (or warp) thread was attached to a second stick. The weaver could now lift one stick and run a filling cross (or weft) thread through one set of alternate threads, then drop the stick and pass his cross thread over the next instead of slowly 'darning' the threads through as before. The two rows of threading and many more would be pushed together to make the close weave of the cloth. The thread was dyed before weaving, so different patterns and colours could be woven in.

A simple kind of cloth could have been made from wool without weaving—felt. To make felt, the wool must be wetted and pressed, wetted and pressed, until it shrinks into an even, smooth material.

By the late Stone Age in Britain men could weave and spin. Wool was the material they used. At the same time in other parts of the world men were using all the other cloths known to man until the discoveries of the last hundred years.

3 Roman in a toga. Even Cincinnatus, a Roman magistrate renowned for his lack of vanity, could get his on only with the help of his wife. In later Rome most citizens only wore the toga to be laid out in on their death bed.

Wool, cotton, linen and silk were all used, whilst even thread of gold was made. Not until the recent invention of rayon, nylon, terylene, orlon etc., have the traditional materials, discovered by ancient man, been replaced in our clothing.

Three thousand years before Christ the Egyptians were making high-quality linen. The nomads beyond the main Nile valley brought them raw wool, but linen and cotton were considered by the Egyptians to be superior to wool, cooler and easier to keep clean. Nobles and pharaohs wore linen of such fineness that it was semi-transparent; remains have been found of linen finer than any woven today.

In the Old Testament of the Bible these 'fine linens with broidered work from Egypt' are mentioned. Some slaves did no other work than weaving and spinning for cloth traders. We find the poor life of such a worker described on a tomb wall: 'His knees are at the place of his heart; he does not taste the air; if he should do but little in a day of his weaving he is pulled like a lotus in the pool. He gives bread to the door keeper in order that he may see daylight.'

Wool and cotton were more often worn by the Babylonians. They lived in the lands between the Tigris and the Euphrates rivers, a rich area that attracted conquerors. These men—Persians—wear what to our eyes is perhaps the most interesting costume of these ancient peoples. For some wear coat and trousers. The coat is like a long tunic, slit down the front, or it may have a sewn in sleeve with a cuff. The trousers are long and drawn in at the ankle.

The most luxurious fabric of all came from further East: silk. In legend the first silk was not woven by ordinary hands but by an Empress of China who made a robe of it for her husband 2,700 years before Christ. But silk was unknown in Western Europe until the Romans spread their conquests across the Mediterranean. The caravan route to the East had become known as the Silk Road because it was used so much for this trade. Not till the sixth century after Christ did the Emperor Justinian bribe two monks to smuggle a number of silk worms' eggs out of China, concealed in their wooden walking staves.

Even before the Roman Empire the Greeks had bought silk from India. They were the chief traders in the Mediterranean: they sold cloth and they bought it. They sometimes bought the silk in return for skilled slaves or even fair-skinned children, captured and sold to the Indian rulers as dancers and musicians. Greek wool was also well known, for the Greeks were thought to have first discovered how to 'full' cloth. Nikias of Megara is said to have found out how to beat and wash the woollen cloth till the grease came out of it and the scaly fibres softened into a smooth surface—the process we call fulling.

The Romans, like the Greeks, never became the most skilled of cloth makers, but for their clothing they could gather together the skilled weavers of a huge empire that stretched to Britain in the North and almost to India in the East. The Romans used so much of the purple dye of Tyre that the shellfish that supplied it almost disappeared; small quantities cost huge prices. Only nobles were allowed by the Senate to wear purple-dyed clothes. Magistrates, consuls and senators were allowed to wear togas with purple borders to show their importance. (This dye is thought to be the same as the rich red still worn by the Cardinals and Popes— rulers of the Church for 2,000 years since the times of the Caesars.) If a general made an entry in triumph into Rome he wore a special toga belonging to the state, made of purple cloth embroidered with gold.

So, by Greek and Roman times all the natural textiles or cloths were known: linen, silk, cotton and wool. Weaving of a high standard had developed, dyes both vivid and delicate had been discovered and gorgeous embroidery and decorations were used.

Further reading.
Oxford Junior Encyclopaedia, Book Eleven, Costume.
Batty: *Man is a Weaver*.
Quennell: *Everyday Life in Ancient Times*.
White: *Everyday Life in Ancient Egypt*.
Place: *Britain before History*.

2 Britons, Saxons, Normans, English

Although Roman soldiers invading Britain saw warriors with bodies tattooed and painted blue with woad, this was only how they appeared in battle. Usually they were clothed. They wore wool and linen, thick and coarse, dyed in bright colours —red, blue, black, green and yellow, as well as the wool colour itself. Often the dyed thread was woven in checkerboard or tartan pattern. Over these clothes the Britons often still wore skins for warmth. Men wore the trousers so despised as barbarian by their Roman conquerors. Rulers and nobles had heavy bracelets and necklets of iron, bronze, gold or beads. The best description of women's clothing at the time of the Roman conquest is that of Boudicca's, a sleeved ankle-length tunic held in with a leather belt, and a cloak over the top.

Julius Caesar noticed that the British of the North and the Midlands were fiercer and still wore skins; the cloth-weaving tribes of the South-east were more civilised.

As the Romans slowly conquered and settled Britain the British style of dress changed, at least for the upper classes who followed Roman manners. But even with Roman-style heating in their villas, the British winter must have been too chilly for draughty togas. The Britons wore a tunic with long sleeves and, in winter, trousers. They also kept the undergarment, a short-sleeved tunic.

When, in AD 410, the legions left Britain to defend Rome against attacking tribes, Britain was invaded. Picts and Scots came down from the North, Angles and Saxons from across the sea. The Anglo-Saxons came first as pirates, thieving and burning, but they settled once they found the land was fertile and could be seized for farming. Their clothes suited their life—easy to make, easy to tuck up and wear when working, but also thick and heavy when needed to keep the wearer warm. Life was hard: only constant work provided enough food to last from year to year and a wet summer and poor crops could cause untold misery. There was little surplus for buying extravagant clothes and cloth. Even linen was too expensive for ordinary people.

The women and children who lived in the little one-room village huts used the wool from their own sheep. Having carded it (i.e. combed the hairs till they were flat and even) they spun and wove the cloth for the simple tunic that was worn for both work and sleep. It was short for men, to keep out of the mud of the fields, longer for women, and worn till it fell to pieces from age and wear or could be passed on in the family. Even a poor woman wore a head covering, often a hooded cloak. Her husband would have a short cloak and either rough trousers held up by strips of material criss-crossed up his leg or wrappings to the knee. These were often discarded for work.

Although any clothing except the garments a man had on his back was a luxury for most people, the richer farmers would wear under-tunics, their wives would embroider wrist, neck, hem and the belt round the waist. The clothes of the greatest leaders were very rich and Anglo-Saxon embroidery was famous, especially for Church garments. When St Cuthbert was buried his body was wrapped in five robes of embroidered silk.

Silk and other beautiful cloth, finer woven than our own, was still being produced in Italy and in some of the towns in France, where cloth had been made in Roman times. Trade, however, was difficult: there were robber barons in Europe as well as ordinary thieves. Merchants found it safer to arrange to meet together at a definite place once a year. They could protect each other and a large gathering of them could pay enough to persuade some great lord to allow the meeting to take place in his lands, at a river or road crossing, and to see that no other landowner attacked them.

King Dagobert of the Franks, in the seventh century, allowed such a 'fair' at the Church of St Denis in Paris in October. He used the money to pay for the embroidered cloths he had given the church. Many other lords found a fair a good way of increasing their income. Great abbeys and churches also encouraged these fairs, partly because they needed to buy beautiful things for their churches. St Cuthbert's feast at Durham led to an annual fair there well before the Norman Conquest. St Bartholomew's Fair was held in London every year until 1855.

Some of the cloth that was sold was embroidered, not only to make fine clothing, but to make wall hangings. It is from one of the early 'tapestries' of this type that we can see the clothes and armour worn not only by Saxon people and soldiers

4 A noblewoman of the ninth or tenth century. Notice the heavy embroideries at the edge and the fine drapery of the kirtle (skirt).

5 Loose braies. *(left)* Braies (underpants) were tied up with cords. They were considered more essential than shirts. The Irish in Richard II's day were noted by the English for not wearing them.

6 Mediaeval women prepare wool for weaving. *(right)* The woman at the front combs the wool after it has been carded (straightened) by the girl in the middle. It is spun on the distaff and, at the back, the loom is being threaded with warp threads.

before the Conquest but the Normans who conquered them. William's half-brother, Odo of Bayeux, is said to have ordered this tapestry to be embroidered for him by Saxons who knew from experience the clothing of both peoples.

After the Conquest the Saxons were the labourers. Their clothing was the hood, tunic, cross-gartered trousers and perhaps leather boots. The Norman lord and his wife would wear more elaborate clothes to show their position. Rich men wore pieces of linen, wool or even soft leather round their legs and feet, held up by strings and tapes, tied to linen underpants or the belt which kept them up. (These were the forerunners of our modern underpants and stockings.) Their soft leather shoes, sometimes coloured and with pointed toes stuffed with wool, were lighter and more comfortable than the peasant's rough boots.

The lady also wore an undergarment, an under-tunic, beneath her gown. The gown was increasingly pulled in by a belt, at waist or hips, under her mantle.

Some gowns began to be made with bodices laced to fit closely; then they were cut to fit, and to fit closely, with seams at the back and front as well as under the arms, even gussets being added to give more room.

Making clothes was now a specialised business quite separate from the making of cloth. A cut and shaped garment needed a skilled hand, a tailor. The first document giving freedom to tailors to practise their trade in a guild (i.e. a group of men skilled in the same trade) was in Hamburg, Germany, in 1152 and in England they must have been developing at the same time. Certainly the shoe-makers had: there was a cordwainer's guild (Cordwainer—shoemaker—from the Cordovan fine goat leather from which they made their best shoes) in London in the reign of Henry I, the son of William the Conqueror. There must have been plenty of work, even though only a few people used money at all and even fewer had it to spend on luxury clothes.

But England was growing richer as her raw wool was sold to the cloth merchants of Flanders and Italy. When foreign weavers came to England from Flanders because of war and trouble in their land Edward III asked their leader John Kemp to teach their skills 'to such of our people as shall be inclined to learn it'. He included Flemish fullers and dyers (see Chapter 6) in his invitation to England. A writer named Fuller later wrote: 'The King observed the great gain to the

7 Two young men. Notice the doublet, waisted and very short. It fastened down the front with lacing, buttons or even hooks and eyes. This one has very ornamental tabs.

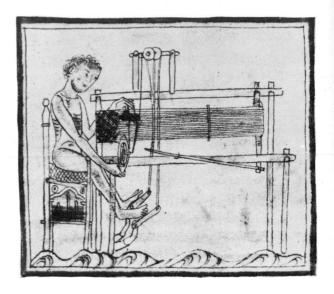

8 Horizontal looms in the Middle Ages. The weaver can raise and lower the alternate threads of the warp threads by means of foot operated treadles. Both hands are free to pass the shuttle through the threads.

Netherlands by the export of this wool, in memory whereof the Duke of Burgundy instituted their order of the Golden Fleece—where indeed the fleece was ours but the gold theirs.'

The best wool was said to come from Shropshire and Herefordshire and sold for 14 marks a sack (one mark was worth 6s. 8d. of their money). The poorer wool of East Anglia was sold for less than four marks. More and more wool was needed not only for the expanding English cloth industry—cloth woven in Stamford was used in Venice—but also to keep up exports of raw wool. Land was taken from corn growing and commons to feed the sheep. Some men, the great wool merchants and clothmakers, grew rich, as we have seen; many men grew poor as they were turned out of their villages.

Further reading.
Ellacott: *Spinning and Weaving*.
The Anglo Saxons. Methuen Outline Series.
Norman England. Methuen Outline Series.
Allen: *Norman England*.
Costume. U.L.P. Discovery Reference Books.
The Norman Conquest. Longmans Then and There Series.
Wool Merchants of the Fifteenth Century. Longmans Then and There Series.
Simpson: *Everyday Life in the Viking Age*.
Rowling: *Everyday Life in Medieval Times*.

3 The Later Middle Ages

Now that far more and finer cloth was being woven in England, Edward III forbade merchants to bring foreign cloth into the country. The 'websters', men who had made simple homespun cloth on their horizontal looms, gave way to workers who specialised, each in his own part of the process. One writer says that, in making the wool cloth, there were 22 separate things to be done, by almost as many workers.

The main processes, however, were washing, carding, rolling the wool into a thick loose string called a 'sliver' for spinning, part bleaching, and then dyeing. The spinner would buy this wool or be given it by a master cloth maker called a clothier, spin it and pass it to the weaver. The weaver then made the cloth which went on to the fuller who cleaned and pressed it. The shearer took it and trimmed it.

9   Priest and knight. One knight here wears chain mail. This was later replaced by plates of metal, as can be seen on the figure on the right. The priest's simple clothes would be replaced by, or covered with, beautiful ones on Feast Days and Holydays.

The most time-consuming process was fulling. The water washed and shrank the cloth which softened and felted a little, then it was 'tented' on 'tenterhooks': that is to say, stretched out on the ground to dry in the open air. This process was often repeated over and over again. The hardest labour was the beating of the wet cloth with hammers, whilst it was wet, to help in the softening process. An easier method of fulling was later used. Heavy hammers, worked by water wheels, beat the wet cloth instead of hand-beating. The water wheels which worked the fulling hammers needed to be sited by fast-running streams if they were to work, not in the towns where the cloth workers were. The merchant, however, found labour both difficult and expensive in the towns.

At first the cloth-makers had joined together in their guilds (small clubs of workers and masters) to fix prices and wages, conditions of work, to keep up the standard of their craft and help each other in trouble. As the masters had grown richer and stronger, the workmen had set up guilds of their own to see that the masters paid enough for the work, did not employ too many apprentices as cheap labour, provided some days as holidays and so on. It was tempting for the cloth-makers to move their work into the countryside to the fulling mills to get their weaving and spinning done there at a cheaper rate.

The guilds, and later on, individual merchants, were able to win more freedom for themselves and for their trade through the Crusades. Richard the Lionheart had said that he would sell London itself if he could find a buyer and many of his followers sold land and freedom to their serfs before they left for the Holy Land. They were particularly glad to borrow money from and sell more rights to rich cloth merchants in order to pay their debts when they came home.

The town workers tried to stop the trade going to the countryside and the smaller masters helped. The cities of Norwich, York, Shrewsbury, the five chief cloth towns of Worcestershire and three of Somerset were strong enough to get a law passed stopping clothmakers from settling in the countryside around them or joining in the cloth trade. But they failed to stop the change. Country cloth was cheaper and country water-wheel fulling was easier.

East Anglia was the chief centre for 'worsted' cloth, the name still used for this type of cloth today. The name came from the little Norfolk village of Worsted where the cloth was first made. Kersey, in Suffolk, gave its name to a narrow woollen cloth which the weavers of Devon also made famous.

There were even some cloth-makers like John Winchcombe of Newbury who had the weaving done on a large scale in his own house:

Within one room, being both large and long
There stood two hundred looms full strong.
Two hundred men the truth is so
Wrought on these looms all in a row.

So the ballad said, describing the woman singing at their spinning in the same place.

When expensive fine cloth was made it was impossible for the craftsman to buy and re-sell the article he had processed. The cloth from the loom was dyed or bleached, it was fulled, it was teased to fluff up the surface with teazles (a plant like a thistle), and then sheared to give an even surface to the finished cloth. One merchant, the clothier, would arrange for the partly finished cloth to be moved from one worker to another, paying for the work done. Many of these clothiers controlled the cloth-making back to the buying of the raw wool. The successful ones became very rich.

Some of them proved good employers but many forced down wages. Today we benefit from their wealth when we see the great church at Lavenham in Suffolk,

11 Shops. Draper's, furrier's and grocer's shops. Beside the draper's are two men, one wearing the long gown, one the short.

built by the Suffolk clothier, Thomas Spring; the stained glass windows at Fairford in Gloucestershire presented by the clothier John Tame; the lovely wool churches of the Cotswolds and East Anglia.

The cloth and wool trade became more and more a source of money and taxes for the King. In 1421 the tax on wool exports produced 74% of all the customs revenue for both imports and exports. Court life was so lavish by the late Middle Ages that even in times of peace Kings ran into debt. The cost and expense of war caused huge debts.

England's part in the Crusades and other wars cost her money but brought many new ideas into the country. Royal marriages kept the country in touch with the ideas of the rest of Europe. Brilliant colours, costly materials, fur, fur linings and edgings, embroideries both silk and jewelled were all worn at Court. Exaggerated styles of dress were copied from the French, gifts of cloth were brought

12 Crossbowman. He replaced the knight as the most important person on the battlefield. He expected to be well paid. The elegance of his suit, mostly blue and white in the painting, shows his wealth.

back from overseas. Despite the disastrous Black Death and the Peasants' Revolt in the fourteenth century, the extravagance in clothes increased.

Dagged edges (zigzag cut edges to material) long streamers, short tunics and close-fitting tights were worn by men, but the most extravagant style of all was the long-pointed shoes; the points sometimes six inches, sometimes 12 to 18 inches beyond the toe. Women's gowns fitted closer and closer, girdled on the hips and buttoned tightly down the bodice. An alternative style of dress was the 'houppelande', a long, heavy robe with wide sleeves that often touched the ground, its wide fulness belted at the waist. This garment was also worn by men over their short tunic and hose. Besides the fur linings and trimmings, embroidery of all kinds and beautiful jewellery, gold and silver bells were placed on chains and sewn to clothes of the more extreme in fashion. Pockets were still unknown: both men and women carried bags which were hung from shoulder or waist.

The most extravagant fashion was perhaps in women's headgear. All hair was pushed out of sight under towering headdresses of different types. The 'henin' is best known; a tall dunce's cap shape with a long veil of fine gauze hanging from it. Sometimes the veil would be woven partly in gold. In France this headdress grew so big that architects had to enlarge the doors of the castle at Blois to enable the ladies to get through. By the early fifteenth century new fabrics had made wealthy women's dresses more luxurious: damask, taking its name from the Saracen town of Damascus, was plain coloured with different patterns woven in, velvet from Genoa, taffeta originally from Persia and other silks. The skirts, gathered into pleats, were often caught up with jewelled hooks of silver and gold.

Kings had their standard-bearers in battle, knights had their heraldic signs painted on their shields or woven on banners to show who they were on the battlefield. At court their servants could be identified by their clothes on which they would wear the heraldic arms of their master. They were wearing the 'livery', as it was called, of their lord. It not only showed whom they served but told people that he would give them protection in time of trouble. Their lord, to identify himself as a great man, would need rich clothing of every type, including the new fabrics brought from the East by the Crusades: damask, gauze from Gaza, baldekyn from Baghdad. Laws were passed forbidding even rich merchants from wearing some of the more exquisite materials.

Even for war armour was chased and inlaid with gold and silver. The clothes underneath were rich to show the owner's wealth and rank, especially as thieves soon stripped the armour from the fallen on a battlefield. The clothes were also stripped off and stolen but this took longer. So extravagant were the clothes worn by the French at Crécy that one French writer blamed the defeat of France on these garments, 'some with over-long sleeves dragging on the ground'. Another said these clothes 'upset the digestion, compressed the stomach and let in the cold'.

Country gentlemen and people far away from the court spent much less on their clothes. We have details of expenditure in the letters of a Norfolk family called

19

Paston, written in the fifteenth century. The women are constantly asking husbands or fathers to buy things we would regard as trivial, such as belts, but they did not always get even these. A schoolboy brother is desperate for 'hose cloth I beseech you—one for the holy days of some colour, and another for the working days how coarse soever . . . and a stomacher and two shirts and a pair of slippers'. On the other hand an alewife (barmaid) wore the same every day clothes for 40 years. We remember that there was no ready-made clothes industry but often we forget that, except in a large town like London, there were few shops.

Working people usually wore wool, russet or kersey, the material was coarse, often spun and woven in the owner's home. Their clothes had very little decoration and if they had any fashion at all it was usually many years behind the time. Many of the little pictures decorating the manuscripts of the 'Holkham Bible Picture

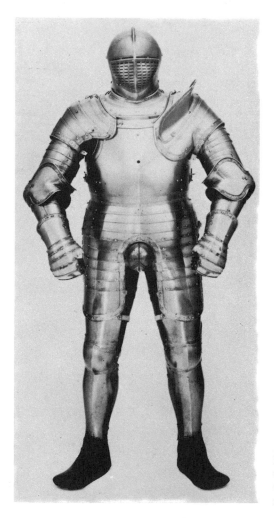

13 Henry VIII's armour. Good armour, heavily engraved, could cost a fortune. It was usually the first thing stolen from the fallen on the battlefield. After gunpowder became common, armour fell out of use.

Book' or the 'Luttrell Psalter' show working people in their ordinary clothes. The men wore belted tunics, sometimes with a garment over the top. Their clothes were made for comfort in work, the tunics were short and, if they were not pulled up round the waist to make it easier to move, they had slits up the sides and often the front. The simplest overgarment was a straight piece of material joined on the shoulders. The 'tabard' was perhaps the beginnings of the smock that country workers wore later on. Few of them went without shoes unless they were very poor. What is surprising is the different kinds of gloves worn for different jobs—anticipating what we call protective clothing today. They were usually of cloth and shaped more like mitts than gloves, with thumbs and one or more fingers separated, often with gauntlets, if the work, such as ploughing, needed it. Round the heads and under the chin a coif was worn, usually a white cloth tied under the chin and fitting like a baby's cap. Out of doors a hood or hat could be worn over the top.

The working man's wife, who would often work with him in the fields in summer, would nevertheless wear skirts that were long and full with a ground-length cloak often hooded to keep out the cold in winter. She might wear a long bibless apron at her work to protect her gown. Chaucer describes one of these aprons, called barm cloths, as 'a barmcloth as white as morning milk'. But although the country girl of the middle ages might try to protect her clothes, she seldom seemed to wear gloves as often as the men.

Sculptures, tapestries, memorial brasses as well as illuminated manuscripts give details of the clothes worn by medieval people: even the constantly changing court styles of the Wars of the Roses are illustrated. By the end of the fifteenth century, however, portrait painters from Flanders and Germany were at work in England painting the outstanding people of the time. From these pictures we can see how the new and lively ideas of the sixteenth century, the time of what we call the Renaissance and the Reformation, changed men's ideas of clothing.

Vasco da Gama's voyage to India in 1498 led to other voyages to the East. The light cotton cloths our ancestors called 'pintados' and 'chints' were imported. More silks became available now that the new sea routes were open. Queen Elizabeth even had silk stockings. Gold, silver and jewels poured into Europe from the Spanish colonies in America, so that even richer and more splendid clothes could be worn and made.

Further reading.
Cunnington: *Costume in Pictures*.
Oxford Junior Encyclopaedia, Vol. VII, Wool Industry (Medieval).
Fraser: *Textiles by Britain*.
Tenen: *This England*.
Price: *Portrait of the Middle Ages*.
Healy: *Town Life*.

4 Tudors and Stuarts

The sixteenth century was a period of change: new lands, new learning, new ways of painting and building, new ways of printing books. At the same time that serfdom (under which a man and his family were in bondage to their lord) was dying out, the wealth from the newly-discovered lands was making a rich middle class of merchants and bankers. When Henry VIII sold up the monastery lands, these new rich and the older established rich clothier families were able to buy country estates and become gentlemen.

To be rich and noble one had to look rich as well. King rivalled king. When Francis I of France met Henry VIII each king tried to outdo the other in the splendour of their dress. The two kings changed their clothes twice each day and neither of them wore any fabric except gold and silver damask. Francis' little niece was married when she was 13. So heavy was the cloth of gold dress stiffly embroidered with silver flowers that she had to be carried into the church. It was no wonder that one writer wrote of the 'fickle headed tailors, who covet to have several tricks in cutting thereby to draw fond customers to more expense of money' (Harrison, *Description of England*, 1587). Fashions changed. 'All manners of attire come first into the city and country from the court, which, being once received by the common people and by very stage players themselves, the courtiers justly cast off and take new fashions.' Elizabeth left over 1,000 dresses when she died. It was a German father and his son who perhaps carried this vanity to extremes. They had their portraits painted in each new set of clothes. There are 140 of these portraits.

The most unusual part of the costume of this time was the ruff. The frill at the neck of the shirt which Henry VIII and his subjects had worn embroidered with gold had grown wider and wider. Becoming still larger, it then became a separate pieces of clothing. When the largest ruffs were worn, long-handled spoons were were necessary if the wearer was to eat. Margaret of Valois, a French princess, solved this problem. She wore a lowcut neckline, with her ruff cut away in front and worn high behind her head at the back.

Two new things, starch and lace, probably helped the rise in popularity of the ruff. Queen Elizabeth had hers starched by a Flemish woman who knew the 'mysterie' of the new starching and charged heavily to teach anyone else her trade. Mrs Turner, who was able to starch ruffs yellow, was found to be a murderess and yellow ruffs became less popular!

Lace-making, a new art, probably from Italy, had become as popular as embroidery. The most expensive lace came from the Netherlands, probably because their linen thread was the whitest and the finest. Lace could be made at home, but gold lace to trim court gowns and doublets was expensive, yet Henry III of France was said to have worn on one occasion 4,000 yards of gold lace on his clothes.

Much of this lace and sumptuous cloth had to be imported from abroad to the annoyance of the Government. Elizabeth had so many silk clothes that she had a 'silk mistress' whose job was to look after them. Silk cloth came from Spain and Italy, but the Queen much preferred her subjects to wear English-made woollen cloth. When there was trouble in Flanders, English rulers such as Elizabeth encouraged the clothmakers to come and settle in England. They were even offered five years free from taxes.

Although the English cloth-makers disliked the foreigners, the new skills they brought improved English cloth and even revived the trade in towns like Norwich. In 1575 the Flemings introduced a new type of cloth called 'bombazine', part silk, part linen and cotton, a cloth for which the town became famous. When Antwerp, the chief cloth town of Flanders, was sacked it was said that a third of its manufacturers and merchants fled to England.

Two other new inventions came into cloth and clothing history at this time, the spinning wheel and the stocking-making machine. The latter, made by a clergyman named Lee, was not popular with Elizabeth. Too many of her subjects earned their living by hand-knitting stockings. Lee was forced to take his invention to France. The spinning wheel, however, was already known in Flanders and soon replaced the old distaff and spindle method used in England.

14 Queen Elizabeth I. Notice the stiff, huge ruff of delicate material. The lavish jewel embroidery made her position and wealth clear.

Many country families came to depend more and more on the spinning earnings of the family. The Merchant Adventurers, a company of merchants, sought to increase England's trade abroad but it was a time of war and trouble overseas. Although weavers often found themselves out of work, there was a steady demand for raw wool. Landlords found it saved trouble to keep sheep on the land rather than grow crops. One or two shepherds could do all the work. When land was used like this, 'enclosed', the cottagers were often forced to leave. The Government was left to deal with this problem as it could.

The sixteenth century is thought of as a period when men wore full, swinging capes, padded wide-skirted jerkins, richly embroidered over-doublets, slashed to show fine linen shirts below or long gowns with hanging sleeves richly trimmed with furs. Tights were worn and breeches, either short and stuffed or later reaching to the knee. Women's clothes had also a full sweeping appearance, rather like a full-rigged ship. Bodices were stiffened with whale-bone and steel rods (busks), pointed at the waist, with low-cut necklines supporting huge ruffs which rose above full embroidered sleeves padded at the shoulder. The wide skirts were held out with layers of petticoats, heavy and hot, till the farthingale, uncomfortable as it was, allowed the stiff skirts to spread even wider but the number of petticoats to be reduced.

Whilst this is true, a much quieter taste in dress was developing. Sometimes it was a great man like the Emperor Charles V of Spain, Austria and the Netherlands who chose to wear plain dark clothes. Generally it was the plainer clothes which were the mark of the new kind of Protestantism, preached by John Calvin. These Puritans, as they came to be called, disliked the vanity of gay and expensive clothes. Plain cloth, dark colours, linen rather than lace were worn.

The clothes in Charles I's court were simpler than those of the sixteenth century but even so, when the King quarrelled with Parliament and the two began a civil war, the two groups were distinguished for many people by the way they dressed. This cannot have been very clear at first, as both sides were often given coloured ribbons to show which side they were fighting for. Later, however, the more Puritan Parliamentary troops wore simple buff leather jerkins over a plain doublet with a linen collar and full breeches. This is still the uniform of the Honourable Artillery Company. The Royalists continued to wear their lace, their short-waisted doublet and soft boots with embroidered or laced boot hose.

Parliament and Cromwell ruled England after winning the Civil War but when Cromwell died the young King Charles II regained the throne. The simple clothing of the Puritan women, the dark, plain frocks, covered often with a white apron to match their white collar and cap, had not been used by many of the great ladies in Cromwell's London. Under Charles, ribbons, laces, bows, feathers —all became popular, and men wore them too! As one Englishman wrote of another in 1661, 'It was a fine silken thing which I espied th'other day through Westminster Hall, that had as much ribbon on him as would have plundered six shops and set up twenty country pedlars; all his body was dressed like a May-pole.'

15 Portrait of a little girl. Notice the padded sleeves, the stiffened bodice and scratchy ruff. Children were dressed as small replicas of their parents once they were out of long baby clothes. Well-to-do boys wore skirts until they were 'breeched' and left the nursery.

Wigs were worn with shaven heads beneath, even muffs and corsets. But at least men's clothes made one useful gain—the pocket, usually placed low on the coat.

The sad aspect of all this splendour was that the clothes got so dirty and often stayed that way, as Pepys tells us in his diaries. Lice were common, especially in the long, heavy hair wigs. Even the rich and wealthy seldom bathed : the poor, often with no water near their homes had little chance even to wash. When a French writer said in 1640 that 'an occasional bath should be taken, the hands washed daily and the face every day or so', he was suggesting a code of polite behaviour, not describing common practice. Even the handkerchief, a new invention, was carried mainly for adornment.

There was often more regard for cleanliness and neatness in servants' dress. Early in the seventeenth century John Harington, who had been tutor to James I's daughter Elizabeth, put down a rule that servants should be fined 6d. for a dirty shirt on Sunday or a missing button. For many this would be half a day's pay or more. Nobles still kept huge numbers of servants (the Duke of Bedford still had 250 on his Woburn estate in 1914) and it is mostly from estate records that we find prices for an earlier date :

'For two shirts for the little page   7s. 6d.

For two periwigs for my lady's page £2 0.0.

In the sixteenth century a well-to-do tradesman's wardrobe was listed as:

'His apparayle

3 bands (collars)

a gowne

2 clokes

a pair of breeches

2 pair of stockens and a hatt.   Sum £3. 4. 0.   1590'

16 Tailor, late seventeenth century. Much clothing was still made at home but tailoring was, by now, a skilled craft. The tailor cuts out, his apprentice sews. Clothing could be so expensive that Puritans scoffed at the lavishness of many Royalists' garments during the Civil War.

Later, in 1757 it cost the Duke of Bedford nearly £5 each for his postilions' uniforms. Made of the orange cloth of the Russell's livery, each was richly laced with gold and velvet and had nearly a hundred gilt buttons, but even so the cost represented the wages for 50 working days of a highly skilled carpenter. On the other hand, the 'link boys', who would run by your side and light your way home to your door for a halfpenny, are usually described as wearing rags.

Further reading.
Price and Mather: *A Portrait of Britain under the Tudors and Stuarts.*
Allen: *Clothes.*
Allen: *The Spacious Days of Queen Elizabeth.*
The Sixteenth Century. Allen and Unwin Picture Source Books.
The Elizabethan Court. Longmans Then and There Series.
Dodd: *Life in Elizabethan England.*

5 The Making of Cloth

Hand-made cloth was produced in different ways in the various areas of England. In the Yorkshire farms a woollen cloth was made entirely in the home of the master weaver. His wife, children and maidservants spun the thread on spinning wheels, every spare hand being used, as it took ten spinners to keep a weaver in thread. Unmarried women made their living in this way, hence their name 'spinsters'. The cloth was woven by the men of the house as the heavy loom was hard to work. The master weaver had apprentices and workmen to help him: often he combined both weaving and farming, taking his bales to the cloth hall in Halifax or the other small towns, to be sold, fulled and dyed. It was often rough cloth but serviceable.

Defoe said of the area in 1727: 'we found the country one continued village . . . as the day cleared up we could see at every house a tenter (a frame with hooks to hold the cloth taut to bleach) and on almost every tenter a piece of cloth'.

In the West of England the cloth was made by what would now be called outworkers, people who worked for a merchant or clothier in their own homes. Some spun thread, others wove, while a 'bagman' distributed the raw wool, collected thread or yarn (as spun thread is called), gave the yarn to the weavers and paid for the labour when he collected the goods.

17 Hand wheel spinning. Both women are well dressed and shod. The room has both grandfather clock and pictures. Notice the other cloth-making tools shown. These women are putting into hanks the wool already spun.

18 Samuel Crompton's mule. This picture is quite late (1844) but notice the small child under the frame on the left, the scavenger picking up the cotton waste and fluff out of the way. Bare feet were common as the floors became slippery and the heat was great.

The finest woollens were made in East Anglia, Norwich being the most famous town in the area. Refugees from Holland and France had settled there, bringing their skill in making 'new draperies'. They made not only fine woollens but Norwich crepe—a mixture of silk and cotton, in great demand for funeral wear. Much of the cloth was made in workshops where master, skilled workers and apprentices worked together, often 50 under one roof.

As the country grew richer and trade abroad increased, more and more cloth was needed, and the spinsters could not provide enough yarn for the weavers. Men experimented with machines to make it more quickly. In 1717 two brothers called Lombe had begun to build a five-storeyed silk-mill in Derbyshire, using a water wheel for power and machinery of a type John Lombe had seen in Italy. This early 'factory' had eight large rooms with 460 windows and cost £30,000. It made silk thread. 'One hand will twist as much silk as before could be done by 50 and this in a truer and better manner'. Thomas Lombe died a knight worth £120,000.

Two men, Wyatt and Paul, had invented a spinning machine for wool but it had little success. John Kay in 1733 invented the 'flying shuttle'. Kay was a good mechanic who had already invented a new way of carding wool. His 'flying shuttle' saved the weaver time and labour. The shuttle that carried the weft thread across the web of warp threads had to be passed from side to side of the loom to the width the arms could reach. Kay's shuttle was hit by hammers at either side of the loom, which sent the shuttle backwards and forwards as the weaver jerked a string that connected to them. Wide cloth could now be made by one man, and the weaving needed far less energy. Kay was hounded out of Colchester, Leeds and Bury by angry weavers who thought they would lose their work. He died a poor man.

Another reason why the weavers showed little interest was that even without the speed of the flying shuttle they were constantly unable to work when supplies of thread ran low. James Hargreaves of Blackburn solved this by building a spinning machine that would spin six threads at once—the machine we call the spinning jenny. Usually a spinner used one hand to draw out a thread from the bundle of carded (combed out) wool or cotton. The other turned the spindle on which it was wound. Hargreaves made his machine with a moveable carriage so that threads from the bundles could be drawn, whilst a wheel turned by hand worked a corresponding number of spindles at the other end. The machine could

19 Children at work winding cotton, about 1820. The children seem rather idealised with their almost dancing-pump shoes. The manager or overseer wears not only a fob but stiff high collar and cravat. All is very unlike the details given to the commissioners a dozen years later!

be used in any cottage and it was quickly copied all over Lancashire. As it was easy to make, ten years after Hargreaves' death there were 20,000 of this machine in use. The number of spindles to a machine could be as many as 80.

Weavers still had to tramp from house to house to buy up enough yarn for their looms, as only the hand-made thread was strong enough for warp. Richard Arkwright, a young barber, travelled about the countryside of Lancashire buying the long hair of country girls to be made into wigs. In 1769, with the help of a mechanic, Highs, who had worked for a spinning machine inventor, he introduced the water-frame or roller-spinning machine. It was so heavy and hard to work it had to be powered by a water wheel. The water-frame had four pairs of rollers which took up the carded stuff: as the rollers turned faster and faster, the thread became finer and finer; at the end of the machine it was wound on spindles. The thread was stronger than the jenny thread, so that it could be more easily used: but it had to be made in 'mills' (as the water-wheel factories were called). Later the new steam engine was used; the age of the factory in the clothing industry had begun.

20 Factory weaving. There were still thousands of hand loom weavers for years after this picture in 1844. Men are still being used for the weaving here.

21 Peterloo Massacre 1819. Notice the factory chimneys for the spinning sheds seen in the background. The work-people were told to come in their best wear. The picture is somewhat dramatised, but compare the work-people's clothing with that of the soldiers.

Although the thread was too thick for the weft of many materials it was ideal for stocking makers. Need of Nottingham and Strutt of Derby gave Arkwright money to build his first factory at Cromford, in Derbyshire (1771), on the same river Derwent the Lombe brothers had used. In eight years Cromford had 300 workers and several thousand spindles. At over 50 Arkwright was taking lessons in spelling, but 'what a historical phenomenon is that bag-cheeked, pot-bellied, much-enduring, much-inventing barber', said Carlyle, whilst a famous cotton manufacturer of Arkwright's age, Sir Robert Peel, said, 'We all looked up to him'. Arkwright died, knighted by the King and worth half a million pounds in 1792.

The invention that made thread both fine and strong and so improved on Arkwright's was a machine for the cottage. Samuel Crompton, a Bolton weaver, was the inventor. He wrote of his 'continued endeavour to accomplish the object of my pursuit, which was that every thread of cotton yarn should be (as near as possible) equally good'. His machine combined Hargreaves' moving carriage with the turning rollers of the water-frame and produced the 'mule', a machine which was a cross between the two. So fine was the thread that some called his invention the muslin wheel: English workers could now make cloth that rivalled and surpassed the fine muslins of India.

Although it was invented before 1779 it was only used in cottages for many years. The complicated machine was difficult to make and the change to factory production was always hindered by the shortage of good mechanics able to make the new machines and people skilled enough to use them. In any case,

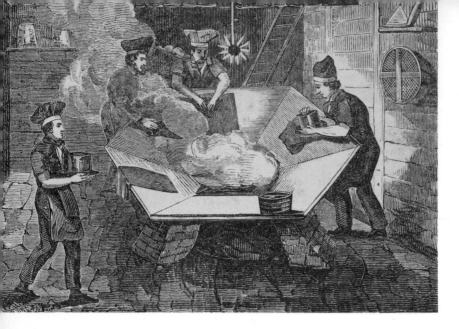

22 Making felt hats in the nineteenth century. Hats were worn by all men. Even factory and mine scenes show caps and hats of one kind or another. They were expensive when new as they were made by hand.

as Crompton's machine was worked by hand, there was little need to use it in factories. But in 1790, William Kelly, the manager of the New Lanark Mills, harnessed the 'mule' to water power. Even so, the mule needed highly skilled workmen to tend it. Mule spinners knew they could not be replaced by unskilled labourers and demanded high wages. In 1830 Richard Roberts invented the 'self-actor' mule, which could be looked after by women and children. In 1832 another machine was invented by an American named Jenks—the ring-spinning machine.

In the face of competition from the factories, the cottage spinning industry began to die out, and more and more cotton spinning centred on Lancashire where the climate was suitable for spinning fine thread. Moreover the steam engine had been used in textile factories since 1785 and coal from the Lancashire mines for fuel was nearby.

Although men fought against the new spinning mills, at least they kept many weavers in work now that the thread was plentiful. But although raw cotton imports from America had increased ten times between 1780 and 1800, the hand-loom weavers were determined to cling to their hand-looms. In 1785 Cartwright, a clergyman, made a loom that was worked by power. Clumsy and large, it depended on weights and springs to work. It was hard to make and complicated to use. The first large factory for 400 of these looms was burnt down by angry weavers in Manchester in 1792. Hand-weavers for a brief period got such good prices for their cloth, especially fine cloths which sold at 3s. 6d. a yard in Bolton, that some walked the streets on holidays with £5 notes stuck into their hat-bands.

In 1803 John Horrocks of Stockport made an all-metal power loom but the hand-loom weavers who desperately tried to destroy the machines were prepared to work for next to nothing rather than give up their independence. In 1830 there were still about 200,000 hand-loom weavers left in the cotton trade, some working for as little as 7s. a week. There were many more still working in the Yorkshire woollen industry till the middle of the nineteenth century.

These inventions for cotton would not have spread so rapidly if Eli Whitney, a young American, had not invented the cotton gin in 1792. The gin tore the fibre away from the cotton seed, a job that had taken a slave one day for one pound of cotton.

Wool cloth manufacture in factories came later. Apart from the many regulations about its use the fibres themselves were more difficult to handle, but there was a worsted (long thread wool) spinning mill on the banks of the Wharfe in Yorkshire in 1787. Benjamin Gott built a large factory outside Leeds in 1792, using a Boulton and Watt steam engine for power, but many of the spinning and weaving machines inside were worked by hand. Linen was even later in factory production. Maberley and Company set up a factory in Aberdeen for 200 power looms in 1824, but even today some linen is still woven by hand.

The price of cloth fell, especially that of chintzes and muslins, as cotton adapted so easily to factory production. Robert Owen, a draper's assistant who became the owner of a huge cotton mill wrote:

'When I first went to Mr McGuffry (the draper) there were no other muslins for sale except those made in the East Indies and known as East India Muslins: but whilst I was with him Mr Oldknow began to manufacture a fabric which he called British Mill Muslin . . . less than a yard wide . . . which Mr McGuffry resold to his customers at half a guinea per yard. It was eagerly sought for . . . much better quality may at this time be bought by the poor at two pence per yard.'

Change of fashion helped to bring this particular price·down but the fall was dramatic. For the first time in history cloth was cheap, even the poor could afford to buy some of it.

Further reading.
Humphreys: *The Industrial Revolution.*
Davies: *Living through the Industrial Revolution.*
A Textile Community in the Industrial Revolution. Longmans Then and There Series.
A Border Woollen Town in the Industrial Revolution. Longmans Then and There
    Series.
Crowther: *Six Great Inventors.*
Allen: *The Nineteenth Century.*
Hill: *British Economic and Social History.*
Vale: *The World of Cotton.*

6 Bleaching and Dyeing

The cloth towns grew. A town like Bradford in Yorkshire owed its growth to the coming of the machine age in woollen production. In 1800 it had one spinning mill and 13,000 inhabitants; 50 years later its population was over 100,000 and there were about 130 mills with power-driven machinery. Between 1821 and 1887 the English cloth factories turned out over 105 million miles of cloth!

If more and more factories were needed to meet the demand, more and more bleachfields were needed to whiten the cloth, new dyes to dye it faster and new methods of printing it.

Land was needed for bleachfields wherever there was a cloth industry. Usually the cloth was wetted in what was called leys and then soured in buttermilk or diluted sulphuric acid and left on tenterhooks to the bleaching action of sun and rain. This was the method used for centuries. It was slow work. The yarn itself was often bleached. In the linen industry the finer cloths, the lawns and cambrics, were bleached in the cloth. These are the directions given for bleaching:

> The yarn is soaked about nine hours in cold water. This is run off and fresh water is added till the loose dirt is removed. It is then wrung dry and put to dry in the bleaching yard. The yarn is then heated with lye of ashes and heated by a slow fire to the boil. Boil three hours. Rinse well and wring. Bleach the yarn three or four days, watering during exposure. The yarn or cloth is then soaked again in warm lye. As the cloth becomes whiter use weaker lye. Again expose to the weather seeing that the yarn does not dry between operations.

It was not surprising that even the cheapest form of bleaching cost 2d.–3d. a yard in eighteenth-century Scotland. The cloth was often then sent to London for printing!

John Roebuck made a bleach from dilute sulphuric acid which replaced the milk and made the bleaching shorter and cleaner. He set up works in Scotland but a fellow-Scot, Charles Tennant, managed to make a powder from the dangerous chlorine bleach discovered by a Frenchman. As a powder it was far easier and less dangerous to store and use. He was helped by Charles Macintosh and later built the largest chemical works in Europe. Bleachfields now were no longer needed as the following advertisement shows:

> Raikes, Near Bolton, April 7th 1789. As it has been industriously reported that I am quitting the business of bleacher, I think it necessary to step forward and thus publicly to declare that so far from my quitting the business, I have lately made an engagement for an establishment in the chemical mode of bleaching, which will enable me to return all goods in a short space of time and in condition and colour that shall do us credit. (Advertisement by John Horridge.)

23 Messrs. Monteith's bleachfields near Glasgow, nineteenth century. The Government encouraged the building of special bleachfields to encourage the textile industry. Notice the factory chimneys with smoke pouring out in the background, also the fact that this was regarded as mainly women's work.

'Spinning, weaving, bleaching and printing' were the four stages Sir Robert Peel gave to Parliament as essential in the making of cloth, in this case cotton cloth. Printing was the one least improved in the late eighteenth century. Printing depended on good dyeing and colouring. The English dyeing of cotton cloth was so poor that the African natives often refused to take our cloth and insisted on Indian-dyed cotton as ours would not wash. The colours 'ran' in the wash, they would spot in the rain and often they were streaked in the dyeing to begin with. Most cloth was dyed with the extracts of plants such as saffron for yellow, woad for blue, madder for dull red, lichen moss for green and indigo from the East for deep blue.

After the cloth had been bleached, if it was to be dyed a 'mordant' was put on. This chemical fixed the dye on the fabric. Different mordants with the same dye can give different colours. The mordanted cloth was washed and 'dunged' to take off the excess. Cow dung for this was so expensive that calico printers usually kept 20–30 cows for the purpose. 'The brightness of the colours and the purity of the whites always depends on the quantity of the dung employed', said an observer. A new dye, Prussian blue, using dried blood in its manufacture, was being made in Newcastle in 1770 and sold at two guineas a pound.

George Gordon in 1775 found a purple dye could be made from a moss. 35

Although he was bankrupted, the work was carried on near Glasgow in a works where the walls were ten feet high and workers spoke only Gaelic so that the secret should not be stolen. The moss was beaten and stirred in troughs of ammonia made from human urine. About 2,000 gallons of the waste product of the town was used daily. They had casks in the loom shops and collectors carried little pocket gauges to make sure they bought rich urine and not 'a spurious and inferior article'. The urine cost the firm £800 a year.

Red was the most difficult colour. Sometimes West Indian cotton was sent out to Turkey to be dyed 'Turkey Red' with madder. Dutchmen and Danes tried to produce a fast dye. One Englishman even sent out an employee to Turkey to find out the method, but in vain. By 1805 Henry Monteith had bought some works near Glasgow and the goods he sold, dyed deep Turkey Red were known through-out Europe as Monteiths.

Manufacturers like Gott of Leeds wrote down the details of involved chemical and dyeing experiments in their works, but not till 1856 were cheap, bright, fast dyes to become possible after William Perkins made the first dyes from coal tar.

The dye colours had been used in printing, both by hand printing with wooden blocks and by copper cylinders. Some fabric was printed for sale but in the days of block printing it was common for the customer to take her linen or cotton calico to the print shop. There she would choose both the pattern and colour she wanted. Laboriously the pattern would be printed. Bell's cylinders, introduced in 1785, changed this practice. Patterns were engraved on copper rollers which were bored from a solid cylinder like a cannon to prevent their having a join. More than one colour could be printed at one time by the use of several rollers. Although this means of printing allowed large quantities of cloth to be treated at small cost, 'often as little as a penny per yard, including dung, colour, paste and printing, poor printing remained common, colours fugitive, mordants were often omitted and a shower of rain was often enough to remove the design'. The machine could print 5,000 yards a day, but dyes had to be improved.

Not till Perkins, in 1856, discovered his artificial dye, mauveine, was there any improvement. From mauveine many other coloured dyes were developed (see

25 New ideas in dyeing. Instead of stirring the fabric round and round by hand, rollers worked by power took it round.

26 A day dress. This was printed in an English fashion journal in 1841. The shawl might be of silk or wool but the checked crinoline with the white inserts at neck and sleeve would be cotton. Think of the labour in the tucks and frills and the expense of so large an amount of material.

27 Roller printing. Wooden blocks had given way to copper plates for finer impressions when Bell brought in his engraved copper rollers. By the 1830's all but a quarter of calico printing was done on rollers.

Chapter 8). Although bright, they faded in the light and were often spoilt by washing. Greiss, a chemist employed by a Burton brewer, in 1864 found 'azo' dyestuffs which will dye cotton directly in one process. Fading still occurred, but in 1880 a British chemist, Holliday, found a method of fast dyeing (i.e. the dye did not run) on the fibre itself. This is now the generally accepted way of dyeing reds, maroons and other shades. In the early twentieth century a German chemist produced aniline vat dyes which are fast and dye the fabric itself a wide range of colours. One of the jobs of the research chemists in most modern cloth-producing countries is to find more fast and even cheaper dyes or unusual colours.

Further reading.
Oxford Junior Encyclopaedia, Vol. VII, Trade, Industry and Commerce.

7 Eighteenth Century to Regency

The last wig to be worn by a churchman was at Queen Victoria's wedding, but there were great changes in cloth and clothes before this. Printing had made it easier for people to see pictures of the latest fashions, pedlars wandered further afield with their wares and came round more often now that the country was more settled.

At the beginning of the eighteenth century doublets for men finally disappeared, and the long straight coat that had replaced it now had a wide flaring skirt stiffened with buckram. The coats and waistcoats were of fine embroidered stuff, velvets and satins for town life and the evenings. Silk or buckskin breeches were worn with silk stockings and buckled shoes. If a coat did not fit smoothly enough on a fat man's figure he would corset himself in.

Men's clothing had always been as decorative and colourful as women's: whether the embroidered smocks of the farm worker on Sunday or the silks and satins of court life. Fashionable clothes, however, began to change. Riding on horseback was still the usual way for men to travel, and it was often a wet and cold occupation. A wide cape had been the normal wear but this gave way to heavy coats, with cape upon cape over the shoulders to stop the wet getting through. The more capes, the greater the fashion. To make sure that the pantaloons, that had taken the place of knee-breeches, fitted as tightly as possible men of fashion damped them. (Their sisters often damped their muslin frocks to make them cling.)

These dandies were often so extreme in their fashion that they were nicknamed Corinthians, Smarts and Fribbles. Years earlier, when such smartness was thought un-English, they were called Macaronis.

These extreme modes faded under the influence of George Brummell, nick-named Beau because of his elegance. He was said to have three hairdressers, two glove makers and to buy his clothes only from the best and most expensive of tailors. His coats were made by one man, his waistcoats by another and his trousers came from someone else. He made the wearing of trousers instead of breeches correct even in fashionable society. The Prince Regent himself envied his style of dress, his clothes tailored in the plainest but finest of materials. The cloth of his coats was usually dark, perhaps to contrast with the brilliant silks usually worn. More than fit, more even than the style of his beautifully arranged cravats, he valued cleanliness. He not only washed himself but insisted on clean clothes and linen 'country washed' for whiteness and freshness. Brummell's dark coats were likely to look free from smuts, and elegant, longer than pale satins. Towns, even in the early nineteenth century, were dirtier as they were more crowded: when

the railways brought cheap coal for household fuel the town air itself became dirtier. The fashion for dark clothes for men did not reach its height, however, till the factory age of the mid and late nineteenth century.

Ladies of fashion had discovered the new, light cotton fabrics that the East India Company had been used to import for bed hangings round their four poster beds. Defoe had poked fun at them in the early eighteenth century: 'Such is the power of Mode we saw persons of quality dressed in India carpets, which but a few years before their chamber maids would have thought too ordinary for them: the Queen herself at this time was pleased to appear in China silks and calico.' Not only were the wool cloth makers angry, a thriving silk industry had grown up mostly in London, using the skills learnt from French refugees at the end of the seventeenth century. Fine printed cotton could ruin this trade in Spitalfields silk.

In the end Parliament forbade the use of India cottons and threatened a fine of £200 if they were imported. Now they tried to make the Indian style cotton-printed cloth in England. Silks and taffetas and fine woollen cloth however still kept their popularity as the English prints did not keep their colours well: the cloth makers had not mastered the art of fast-dyeing the cloth. The ban on printed cotton was raised in 1774, by which time the revolution in the weaving and spinning of cotton was well under way.

	£	s.	d.
A smock of Cambrick Holland, about 3 ells and a half at 12s. per ell	2	2	0
Marseilles quilted Petticoat, 3 yds. wide and a yard long	3	6	0
French or Italian Silk quilted Petticoat, 1¼ yds. deep and 6 yds. wide	10	0	0
Mantua and Petticoat of French Brocade, 26 yds. at £3 per yard	78	0	0
French Point Lac'd Head, Ruffles and Tucker	80	0	0
Stays covered with Tabby (English)	3	0	0
French Necklace	1	5	0
Flanders laced Handkerchief	10	0	0
French or Italian Flowers for the Hair	2	0	0
Italian Fan	5	0	0
Silk Stockings, English	1	0	0
A Girdle, French		15	0
Shoes, English	2	10	0
A Cambrick Pocket Handkerchief		10	0
French Kid Gloves		2	6
A black French silk Alamode Hood		15	0
A black French lac'd Hood	5	5	0
Imbroidered Knot and Bosom Knot, French	2	2	0
Hoop-Petticoat covered with Tabby	2	15	0
	£210	7	6

Women had worn hooped dresses with the skirts looped up to show a satin petticoat and a low-cut bodice draped with a soft piece of cloth called a fichu. In the middle of the eighteenth century the material at the back of the dress was allowed to fall straight from the shoulders to the floor. The hooped skirt was still wide enough for staircases to be designed to fit them. A folding hoop frame became fashionable; its owner could lessen the width of her skirts when this became necessary. The fashion for lace, copied by the English ladies of fashion from the French court, led to such a demand for this expensive material that an Englishman named Hammond invented a machine to make tulle. This cloth, lighter and airier than either muslin or lace, was so popular that it was often made into little aprons to be worn for effect by ladies who would never be expected by anyone to work.

The lighter cottons and silks showed to advantage in a less stiff style; by the 1780s rich Englishwomen were adapting their clothes to a simpler line, hoops gave way to a kind of bustle, a simple flowing skirt, a bodice with elbow length sleeves and a low round neck. As the lighter materials were cheaper, their owners could buy more dresses; they were washable which meant the colours could be lighter. In 1793 a Mrs Thrale wrote: 'Muslins that my mother paid eighteen or twenty shillings a yard for may now be had for a Crown'. In a sale at The Pantheon Family Warehouse in Oxford Street in 1806 they were selling off '900 muslins at 1s. 6d., 1s. 10d. and 2s. per yard, 50 very curious at 2s. 6d.' So popular did these simple muslins become during the Napoleonic period that the Director of one famous costume museum noted that out of 70 dresses they have for the period 1800–20 38 were white, 14 more have a white ground.

Up till about 1810 the well dressed woman was still lacing herself into her corsets to hold her bosom high and her simple dress still kept her warm because of the several petticoats below. The mode for very fashionable ladies after this date seemed to need less and less in the way of a petticoat, so much so that one poet wrote:

Like Mother Eve our maids may stray unblam'd
For they are naked and are not ashamed.

With this lack of petticoats a woman of fashion would wear knickers, a garment usually only worn by professional dancers. Poorer men and women could not follow the extravagant modes of the rich nor pay for the splendid materials and the hours of hard labour used in making them. The townswoman would copy the new simple style as best she could with a shepherdess' straw hat and a draped fine linen scarf at the neck. In the pictures of country servant girls they seem to have skirts that hang without hoops and wear mob caps on their heads. The town maidservant was far smarter. The mistress of one of these maids wrote about her

29 Seamen and girls. Another picture, a little later, shows a seaman wearing a petticoat still common at sea at a time when ordinary seamen supplied their own clothes. This sailor wears an unusually good coat with cuffed, buttoned sleeves.

in 1722: 'she had not liv'd with me three weeks before she sewed three Penny Canes round the bottom of her Shift', to serve as a hooped petticoat. When waists were high at the end of the eighteenth century they would tie their apron strings high, under their bosoms:

> *The servant girls they imitate*
> *The pride in any place, Sir,*
> *And if they wear a flowered gown*
> *They'll have it made short waist, Sir.*

Or so the popular song said. A letter to *The Times* in 1795 complains of the waste of flour entailed in the starching of servants' white dresses and muslin kerchiefs. Some employers complained of the cost of washing these printed cottons.

Clothes cost so much when the making of the cloth and the garment itself was by hand. The coat might be adorned with buttons of silver, the waistcoat heavily embroidered, but the clothes they adorned would be made to last a lifetime. A coat would cost as much as a suite of furniture. When embroidered 'muslin-worked robes worth Six Guineas' were being sold for two in the Pantheon sale a knee hole writing table could be bought from a reputable carpenter for from £2 8s. to £5 2s., a four-pound loaf of bread was about 1s. 6d. and farm labourers were earning less than 10s. a week whilst sailors were paid 19s. a month. Ship's chaplains were paid £12 10s. a month. Earlier, Dr Johnson had been told that he could live in London on £30 a year. He allowed £10 for clothes and linen, although he lived in a garret at 18d. a week. Yet Johnson was well known for his poor clothes and grubby linen. When John Jervis, later to become an admiral, entered the Navy in 1747 his angry father was only willing to give him '£20 in his pocket an' a suit of clothes'. In his old age he recalled how his first coat hung down to his heels because he bought it second hand and how he was compelled to make a pair of trousers out of his bed linen. When a brewery in the twentieth century sent its draymen on parade in the livery of the 1750s, coat, hat, breeches and buckled shoes cost £150 each man in our money. Apart from pictures we have few examples of the clothes of ordinary working people before the nineteenth century. They were worn till they fell to pieces; even then the cloth was cut up and used again wherever there was any wear left in it.

Even so, foreigners in the early nineteenth century noticed the neat clothes of the English countryfolk. One commented on the scarlet cloaks and the black silk bonnets of the country women in the market towns, 'When a class, so inferior, is so well dressed who can doubt of the prosperity and comfort of the nation to which it belongs'. Under the cloaks they wore grey gowns and checked aprons. The

30 Diana, Viscountess Crosbie, (left). The eighteenth century lady is painted standing in the country. She would be unlikely to walk there. Country ladies might walk but great ladies were expected to use a carriage. Walking out only became fashionable for ladies in the late nineteenth century.

31 Tanning leather. After scraping (at right) the soaked skins were 'baited' in pits of dog or bird muck in water. Leather was popular for breeches as well as gloves, shoes, boots, aprons, etc., in the eighteenth century. Long after the breeches passed out of fashion they were eagerly sought after by second-hand merchants for the 'Irish Trade'.

miners of the Newcastle area had striped wool stockings and caps of a traditional type. Farm labourers wore a smock frock usually bleached a light fawn with washing and weather, or blue or olive green coloured with vegetable dyes. They wore this over leggings and breeches. One writer says: 'Most Englishmen at their callings dressed in clothes of the stoutest quality; yeomen in fustian coats, corduroy breeches and ribbed worsted stockings, brewers in quilted coats of immense thickness: fishermen in striped jerseys, grey aprons, leather leggings, top boots and fur lined caps: firemen in horse hide lined with leather, quilted with wool and strengthened with metal. A Lancashire handloom weaver's garb was a green woollen waistcoat with a silk neckerchief, his wife's a white linen mob cap with cotton gown and petticoat, a striped calico apron and black hose and shoes.'

One Lancashire girl described her best outfit which she wore for the holiday or 'wakes'. It was 'a gown made with tucks and flounces, new shoes with stand up heels, new stockings with clocks, a tippet with frills all round, many a string of necklaces, and a bonnet made by the new mantua maker, the prettiest as ever were seen, with a sky-blue underside and pink ribbons.' This sounds so smart that it must have been in the few years when hand-made thread and cloth was in great demand at home and abroad and the factory machine had not taken over.

Knee-breeches might be out of fashion, (the French Revolution scorned some types of them) but the ordinary man found them the most useful garment to work in, especially with gaiters over the top for more protection. Ordinary sailors at the time of Trafalgar had no uniform clothing. They might have a blue jacket with buttons, waistcoat and trousers were white or fawn with stripes of red or blue. The trousers were wool in the Channel Fleet, but of thinner material in the Mediterranean. In any case they barely reached the ankle so they could be rolled up on the wet decks. Their shirts were plain, checkered or striped and the black neckerchief was usually tied round their heads to stop the sweat running into their eyes when they were in battle. They wore straw hats, of all sizes in height and brim, sometimes they had them made of leather or painted canvas to keep the wet out. On special occasions they would trim them with ribbons and flowers.

Sailors would often make their own clothes, especially as many were sail makers and handy with a needle 'They were issued with twelve yards of duck, thread and needles, and a black silk handkerchief. A brass nail was driven into the deck at three and six yards as a guide for measuring . . . you would see fellows run to the galley fire, burn a stick, down on deck, dot off the shape and commence work at once.' The officer's clothes were far more carefully made, and expensive. On one

32 Country gentlemen and labourers. Leicestershire rams shown here were a new breed that provided both better wool and meat. They were first bred by Robert Bakewell. Notice the gentlemen's clothes and the smocks and neckerchiefs of the farm workers.

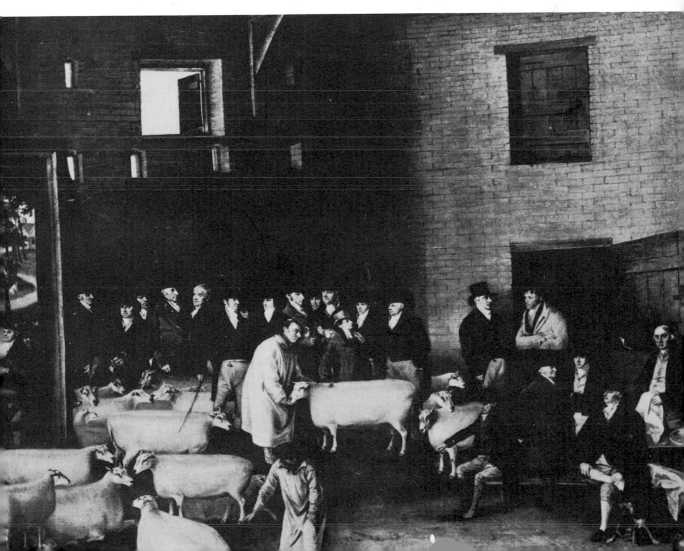

crack ship 'even the midshipmen in 1815 were wearing cocked hats, tight white pantaloons and Hessian boots with gilt twist edging and a bullion (real gold) tassle'. It must have been a crippling expense for the parents of these young boys. Fortunately, when the Duke of Clarence, one of the King's sons tried to have gold topped boots allowed he was unsuccessful.

Men's fashions in the eighteenth and early nineteenth centuries were to be seen at their brightest in the army. Waterloo has been described as the best-dressed battle in history. A foreign marshal pointed out to the English during the Napoleonic Wars 'a grossness as regards the dress of your cavalry. I have seen prisoners so tightly habited that it was impossible for them to use their sabres with facility.' Two years before Waterloo, when fighting at Bayonne, Wellington 'on looking around, saw to his surprise a great many umbrellas with which the officers protected themselves from the rain which was then falling. Arthur Hill came galloping up to us saying "Lord Wellington does not approve of the use of umbrellas during the enemy's firing, and will not allow gentlemen's sons to make themselves ridiculous in the eyes of the army." '

If an officer's clothes were so valuable that he could try and protect them from rain in the middle of enemy action, the cost of the clothing of the wives of the nobility may be imagined. Just after Waterloo, 1815, Lord Grey said he would not dress Lady Londonderry for £5,000 a year. Her handkerchiefs cost 50 guineas the dozen. Yet her coal-owner husband had small children in his mines who worked all day, six days a week for a wage of 3s.–4s. The dandy of the time would devote his life to appearing beautifully clad at the right places. Clothes were the man and marked each person's place in society. Even one of the working class reformers at the trials, after the great reform meeting at Peterloo in 1819 had been broken up, said that when the witnesses got together at the trial the 'broad cloth men and the narrow cloth did not mingle'. Broad cloth could only be made if two skilled workmen worked together at the loom, so it was expensive. Narrow cloth was often rough and homespun as it could be made by one weaver on the kind of machine that fitted into a cottage.

New inventions were, however, already under way that would so reduce the price of cloth that gradually these distinctions would be impossible to draw.

Further reading.
Barfoot: *Everyday Clothing in England.*
Allen: *Eighteenth Century England.*
Harrison: *Picture Source Books for Social History.*
London in the Eighteenth Century. Longmans Then and There Series.
Quennell: *History of Everyday Things in England.*
Williams: *Life in Georgian England.*
White: *Life in Regency England.*

8 The Victorian Age

George IV, Victoria's uncle, spent a fortune on his clothes when he was Prince Regent. Thackeray said of him 'But a bow and a grin. I try and take him to pieces and find silk stockings, padding, stays, a coat with frogs and a fur coat, a star and a blue ribbon, a pocket handkerchief prodigiously scented, one of Truefitts best nutty brown wigs reeking with oil, a set of teeth and a huge black stock, under-waistcoats, more underwaistcoats and then nothing.' We still have a sale list of his wardrobe (all his clothes) : it sold for £15,000, second hand.

Whoever bought his clothes would have bought valuable materials and embroideries; for instance, one hat had been decorated with 5,000 steel beads. What is surprising is that his clothes were sold off so openly, but everyone was used to both wearing and trading in second-hand clothes.

Weaving and spinning had made cloth cheaper, they had also given men and women factory work away from home. Some ready money was now available in their weekly wages: in good times a little part of it could be put aside for clothes. The long factory hours left little time for making clothes, or even learning the skills of patching and mending, when girls went to the loom and the mine at an early age.

In Manchester in 1814 it was said:

> The clothing of the working people, in the majority of cases is in very bad condition. . . . Wool and linen have almost vanished from the wardrobe of both sexes. Shirts are made of bleached or coloured cotton goods; the dresses of the women are chiefly of cotton print goods, and woollen petticoats are rarely to be seen on the wash line. . . . Fustian has become the proverbial costume of the working men who are called 'fustian jackets' and call themselves so in contrast to the gentlemen who wear broad cloth. . . . The Irish have introduced the custom, previously unknown in England, of going barefoot. In every manufacturing town there is now to be seen a multitude of people going about barefoot, and their example is gradually being adopted by the poorer English.

Cheaper ready-to-wear clothes could now be bought, in 1867 a sale of underclothes was announced in the *Illustrated London News* of 700 very fine flannel petticoats in scarlet or white, 1,000 camisoles; tucked drawers, long cloth tucked petticoats etc. Although these were for a better-class trade, ready-made clothes were becoming more common. It was still, however, the normal thing to make them or have them made. Second-hand clothes were not easily available in the industrial towns where most people were also short of money, nor would the pride of many working folk have allowed them to buy clothes. Moreover, in days when infectious diseases were so much feared and the Prince of Wales (Edward VII)

33 The coster boy and girl Tossing the Pieman. Coster boys reckoned to be smart dressers when they had the money. They were especially proud of their silk neckerchief, called a 'King's-man'.

himself was made ill by infection carried in a suit of clothes stitched in the East End of London, second-hand clothes had their own terrors.

Nevertheless, one of the chief sources of ready-made clothes for the poor, at least in big towns like London, was the second-hand, third- fourth- or even fifth-hand clothes sold there. In the country they were sold at fairs. 'Rag Fair' is a name still given to cloth markets, and it well describes the lowest end of the trade in those days.

In London the buying and selling is well described by the reporter Mayhew. 'Connected with the trade and central market for old clothes are the adjoining streets of Petticoat Lane.' He describes how the clothes have first come through The Old Clothes Exchange. The Exchange had been so noisy that the East India Company, who had warehouses nearby, complained; sometimes it took 200 constables to keep order. The houses and shops had been bought by a Mr L. Isaac, who dealt with all the cast off clothing of the city, he would buy a single hat or an entire wardrobe. Another Exchange, Simmons and Levys, only opened in the morning to buy wholesale the unredeemed clothes left as pledges to the pawnbrokers:

But Petticoat Lane is essentially the old clothes district. Embracing the street and alleys adjacent to Petticoat Lane and including the rows of old boots and shoes on the ground, there is perhaps two or three miles of old clothes. . . .

Gowns of every shade and pattern are hanging up. Dress coats, frock coats, great coats, livery and game keepers coats, paletots, tunics, trousers, knee breeches, waistcoats, capes, pilot coats, working jackets, plaids, hats, dressing gowns, skirts, Guernsey frocks, all are displayed.

Garments were sold and resold.

Even if many of the clothes came from pawnshops or were the cast-off clothes given to their servants by well-to-do employers, many too came from far more doubtful sources. Fagin, in Oliver Twist, teaches the boys to steal handkerchiefs, but this seems as nothing compared with child-stripping: 'old hags . . . accost tidily dressed children with good boots and clothes . . . give them a halfpenny or some sweets . . . and take off the articles of dress.' Stealing linen exposed to dry was another well known trick. Mayhew also describes 'little ragged boys . . . loitering about half naked or fluttering in shreds and patches . . . these area divers go down into areas and enter the kitchen . . . steal anything they can find such as clothes, wet or dry linen. . . .'

Nevertheless working-class people could buy a few clothes. The young village girl going 'into service' ('service'—becoming a servant—was still one of the chief occupations of the country) went with a stock of working and afternoon dresses.

34 Vagrants in the casual ward of a workhouse. Mayhew described her 'torn old cotton gown, the pattern hardly discernable from wear . . . shawl patched and mended . . . old broken boots and ragged stockings.'

The material, often printed calico, would perhaps be bought from a pedlar and made up at home. Richer people would have a dressmaker come by day or stay a few weeks to fit out the family. There were travelling tailors. Sewing was still a painful process. Great ladies had their own maids to keep and repair their clothes and make the simpler garments, but each garment was still made individually, cut out laboriously and hand stitched.

Many seamstresses and tailors were needed to meet the demands of the ever-increasing population. Some of the poorest paid of these were the women who endlessly sewed shirts as the poet Hood describes them in *The Song of a Shirt*. The same system of cheap work by women in their own homes continued even when the sewing machine came in. Miss Rose, a Factory Inspector, described in 1907 the conditions of one of these shirtmakers who told her: 'In London the rate of pay for common export shirts with collar band only is 10d. a dozen, that is making throughout. . . . she made shirts at 8¾d. a dozen and some were 6d. a dozen. She thought she made about the same on the 6d. a dozen as she did on the 8¾d. a dozen because more work had to be done to get the higher price.' Charles Kingsley, the author, wrote a pamphlet in the 1850s *Cheap Clothes and Nasty* about the 'sweating' of tailors in the East End workshops of London. His novel *Alton Locke* (1850) gave more details. He 'drew a picture of sweat shop and garret and cellar where consumptive men and women plied their trade, but showed the shivering wretches using the garments they were stitching to cover their naked limbs'. The poorly lit, tiny airless workshops and long hours made consumption and blindness the diseases of tailors. Military tailoring was worst for blindness, the glare of the scarlet often being fatal for the eyes.

35   Seamstress 1849. Seamstresses were often paid only threepence per shirt, sometimes less by the dozen. It was known to be a sweated industry and was shown as this in a Punch cartoon of 1850. 'Needle money' is the opposite of 'pin money'—the Victorian name for a rich woman's pocket money.

NEEDLE MONEY.

Comparative Prices
1840 St. James' Street, London, tailor's Bill
(This would be top quality and price)

	£	s.	d.
Brown Mackintosh Cloak with pink Velvet Collar	5	15	6
Superfine olive Dress Coat	5	0	0
Black Cashmire Waistcoat	1	7	6
Black Cashmire Trowsers	2	12	6

Yeomen Farmer's bills (middle class) in author's possession

1848 Hotel Bill

3 Dinners and Ale	7	6
2 Teas	3	6

1864 Bill for a Funeral Wake

1 lb. Butter	1	3
Plum Cake	3	0
1 lb. Cheese		$5\frac{1}{2}$
1 pint Brandy	4	0
1 pint Rum	3	0
Leg of Mutton per lb.		$9\frac{1}{4}$
12 days Board and Room	5	0

1865 School Bill

	£	s.	d.
Half year's Board and Tuition	11	11	0
Half year's Washing (Clothes)	1	1	0
Haircutting			6
5 Exercise Books		1	8

Household budgets of a skilled worker's family

	1834	1859
Food	16s. 11d.	18s. 6½d.
Coal and light	2s. 5½d.	1s. 6d.
Clothes	5s. 6d.	3s. 0d.
Rent	3s. 6d.	4s. 0d.
Sundries	1s. 10½d.	2s. 11½d.
	30s. 3d.	30s. 0d.

'Early Victorian England', Homes & Habits, Mrs C. S. Peel.
The two budgets quoted showed that if more had to be spent on food then less
was available for clothes and other 'luxuries'.

36 A room in Holloway's factory. The machines were supposed to work at 800 stitches a minute. Each girl makes the garment, unlike our present mass-production. Notice the bonnets on the wall.

A sewing machine had been invented years before, both by an English shoe-maker and a Frenchman who had used it for Army uniforms. But it was not until Howe, an American, completed his lock-stitch machine and Singer, in 1851, put his machine on the market, that a really efficient machine was produced in large quantities. Factory organisation could develop it, as the hand and treadle sewing machine could be easily adapted to steam. George Holloway and Company were said to be 'the first in the world to sew by steam'. Each machine could produce 150 pairs of trousers a week. In 1856 John Barron's clothing factory in Leeds used sewing machines and three years later they were operating a band saw to cut several thicknesses of cloth at one time, in order to keep up with the demand.

Jane Austen's cry in 1798, 'I cannot determine what to do about my new gown: I wish such things were to be bought ready made', was slowly being met. Most outer clothes in the nineteenth century for middle- and upper-class women were still made at home by private and travelling dressmakers, or dressmaking establishments, whilst their husbands went to their tailors. Clothes production still remained a 'sweated' small-scale industry. It ranged from the Court dressmaker, a little like the smart Madame Mantolini's in Dickens' book *Nicholas Nickleby*: girls in such an establishment could sometimes work 36 hours at a stretch in order to finish clothes for the 'season', during which dresses were needed to wear at Court or at the great balls held in the houses of Society hostesses.

At the other extreme were the cheap one-room East End businesses where a reformer named Beatrice Webb was to find work 40 years later. Often the two worlds met: trouser hands for Savile Row tailors would farm out work to East End garret sweat shops, the East End itself would send work out to the new working-class areas as far distant as Walthamstow: the clothes would then be brought back by 'half-fare children' on the cheap early morning trains into Liverpool Street, near Petticoat Lane.

More and more needlewomen were needed as fashions became increasingly complicated. By the 1850s women's clothes, already stiffened out with six or seven skirts, became even more voluminous. Light steel hoops replaced these underskirts. The 'crinoline' was soon made not only of steel but of whalebone and bamboo. It was worn over a small, wasp-waisted corset and long, fitted drawers. A tiny waist was so valued that in one school 'the girls were sealed into their stays by the headmistress. The stays were only removed for one hour on Saturday so that the girls could wash themselves.'

These clothes made women seem small and helpless, according to the fashion prints. Yet photographs of a type were taken from about the middle of the century and they show many women, including Victoria herself, who look far from being helpless. What these restricting clothes did indicate was the social difference between women able to do so little active work if these clothes were to be wearable, and their more hard-working sisters.

Working girls tried to keep up, however. Before the crinoline they could not have hoped to copy ladies like Lady Aylesbury who in 1842 was wearing '48 yards of material in each of her gowns and . . . a petticoat of down or feathers which swells out this enormous expanse.' The cheaper crinoline style allowed them a chance to copy upper-class fashion. Some factory girls wore the hooped skirt to work; in 1863 a Staffordshire pottery firm said that pottery worth £200 had been smashed in one year by the wide skirts of their workers.

Although clothes for women were darker by day than the light fabrics worn around 1800 they must have been vivid to see by night. Under the candlelight or the new gas lighting were to be seen colours that had not been dyed before, or had been so expensive that few could afford them. In 1856 W. H. Perkin found a way of making a violet dye cheaply from coal-tar products. Other bright colours followed as a result of this discovery and others made in 1864 by the brewer's chemist Mr Greiss.

The most elegant of gowns, however, still came from Paris. Fashionable ladies who went there could see the clothes not only in drawings or displayed on small model dolls as before, but worn by actual women. These first 'models' could be seen at the fashion house of Charles Worth, an Englishman who was dressmaker to the elegant Eugenie, Empress of France. This was far too expensive for even quite well-to-do ladies, but there were alternatives besides the Court dressmakers. New-style shops were appearing like William Whiteley's 'Universal Provider' (1860), a large store in fashionable Bayswater where both men and women could buy clothes and cloth of all types, under the one roof.

37 Wentworth Street, Whitechapel, about 1870. Notice the grown-up clothes the children wear . . . especially the little girls with their hats. This was in the 'second hand' area—see the Army hat and epaulettes hanging up.

Costermonger's Tailor's Handbill advertising his Wares.

ONCE TRY YOU'LL COME AGAIN
Slap-up Tog

and out-and-out Kicksies Builder Mr ——— nabs the chance of putting his customers awake, that he has just made his escape from Russia, not forgetting to clap his mawleys upon some of the right sort of Ducks, to make single and double backed Slops for gentlemen in black, when on his return he was stunned to find out of the top manufacturers of Manchester had cut his lucky and stepped off to the Swan Stream, leaving behind him a valuable stock of Moleskins, Cords, Velveteens, Plushes, Swansdowns, etc., and I having some ready in my kick, grabbed the chance, and stepped home with my swag, and am now safely landed at my crib. I can turn toggery of every description very slap up, at the following low prices for

READY GILT—TICK BEING NO GO.

Upper Benjamins, built on a downy plan, a Monarch to half a finnuff. Slap up Velveteen Togs, lined with the same, 1 pound 1 quarter and a peg. Moleskin ditto, any colour lined with same, 1 couter. A pair of Kerseymere Kicksies, any colour, built very slap up, with the artful dodge, a canary. Pair of stout Cord ditto, built in the 'Melton Mowbray' style, half a sov. Pair of very good broad Cord ditto, made very saucy, 9 bob and a kick. Pair of long sleeve Moleskin, all colours, built hanky-spanky, with a double fakement down the side and artful buttons at bottom, half a monarch. Pair of stout ditto, built very serious, 9 times. Pair of out-and-out fancy sleeve Kicksies, cut to drop down on the trotters, 2 bulls. Waist Togs, cut long with Moleskin back and sleeves, 10 peg. Blue cloth ditto, cut slap, with pearl buttons, 14 peg. Mud Pipes, Knee Caps, and Trotter Cases, built very low.

A decent allowance made to Seedy Swells, Tea Kettle Purgers, Head Robbers, and Flunkeys out of Collar.

N.B.—Gentlemen finding their own Broady can be accommodated.

Explanation:—
   Kicksies—Trousers. Cut his lucky—gone off quickly.
   Kick—Pocket or sixpence. Upper Benjamins—Great coats.
   Monarch, Couter or Canary—One Pound. Finnuff—Five Pound Note.
   Peg—Shilling. Bull—Five shilling piece. Trotter case—Shoe.

Further reading.
Unstead: *The Rise of Great Britain.*
Cootes: *Britain Since 1700.*
Richards and Quick: *Britain 1714–1851.*
Langley Moore: *The Woman in Fashion.*
Langley Moore: *The Child in Fashion.*
Laver: *Taste and Fashion.*

9 Buying and Making

It was not till the factories were turning out goods in plenty that shops like ours today were opened. Stalls and shuttered booths were common in Queen Elizabeth's day, and in large towns the shops had open fronts. Glass was expensive and hard to make in big sheets, but by the eighteenth century there were some little shops with glass windows divided into small panes. Even in 1800 the largest shop in London only had 16 assistants. When new shops opened they expected to sell to the middle and upper classes; H. G. Wells, the novelist, speaking of the 1850s, said that there were few shops for the poor and that his friends' homes 30 years later were equipped with second-hand things.

If clothes were bought new by the country poor (or even by the middle class in some isolated parts), they often came from the Scotch draper or tallyman, a wandering pedlar. Some, in the early days of the factories, made a great fortune, like David Dale, the owner of the New Lanark Mills. The tallyman got his name from the stick or tally he carried to notch up purchases and split as a receipt for part-payment. Some carried their goods on their backs, some were women: in 1801 Parson Woodforde wrote, 'Nancy bought a new Gown of Mrs Batchelor of Reepham who travels about with a Cart'. The new gown would be a dress length not a made up garment.

Market stalls might still sell draperies in biggish towns but the village shop had to serve for most people. It sold everything but was often out of stock! Jane Austen wrote of hers: 'I went to Mrs Ryder's and bought . . . there were no narrow braces for the children and scarcely any netting silk, but Miss Wood, as usual, is going to town soon and will lay in a fresh stock. I gave two shillings and three pence a yard for my Flannel, and I fancy it is not very good.'

38 A woman shopkeeper comes to serve, 1844. Notice the dress of the crossing sweeper and the many-caped coat of the coachman, an earlier style still being worn by many servants up till the 1914 war.

39 A shawl shop in Regent Street, 1866. Notice the enormous crinolines.

The centre of the drapery wholesale trade was in London, near St Paul's Churchyard, where it remained till the Blitz and fire raids of the last war made even old established firms move. The drapery shops were dark inside because of the material on show: 'The doors of the linen drapers are closed by draperies of new muslins and calicoes. Some wags pretend indeed that the tradesman has a motive in these proceedings, the darkening of his premises to prevent keen eyes from discovering coarse threads.'

Some of the shopkeepers from small towns travelled to London to get the latest modes for themselves. The shopkeeper in *Cranford,* a novel of country town life in mid-Victorian days, 'ranged trades from grocer to cheesemonger to man milliner' and pretended he went to London for the fashions he showed each season. The London shopping area was widening. Regent Street, built after Waterloo, had become a fashionable clothes shopping area. Bond Street was for the rich, especially men; Oxford Street dealt in clothing of all types. There were 33 linen drapers, ten straw hat-makers shops, 24 boot and shoe shops, 17 hosiers and glovers in the street as well as furriers, tailors, silkweavers and corset shops.

Open stalls were still common in the area, however. William Edgar slept under his stall at night and so met John Swan who had a stall nearby. This was the beginning of the 150 years-old Swan and Edgar of Piccadilly. When gas lighting came in, the jets were put outside the windows to make the display even more brilliant. People at the time said that silk and woollen merchants goods were too expensive for much competition, but the cheap cotton cloth pouring out of the mills meant cut-throat competition in the shops.

Although bright young men would leave London for shops of their own in other

59

40 A market scene. Preston in the 1850s.

towns, like Robert Sayle who went to Cambridge, few shops had branches. Singer's, with their sewing machines, were the first manufacturers to open up retail shops of their own; by 1877 there were over 160 Singer shops. Their slightly cheaper rivals, Jones, introduced hire purchase.

Although the sewing machines were expensive they were easily used at home. One machine in 1866 was 'unrivalled for family use in dress and mantle making, embroiders as well as sews'. Another one 'tucks, hems, frills, gathers, cords, quilts, braids and embroiders'. There were machines for the factory, for the home, for sewing maids, for visiting dressmakers, for all who could afford. Not only was it possible to have the endless rows of tucks and gathers the costume of the day decreed, but ordinary people with a machine could now keep in fashion. The magazines of the day gave details of cloth and trimming, with pictures of women of the times.

In August 1850 the magazine *World of Fashion*, price 1s., began to include in each month's issue a collection of patterns, 'in order that ladies of distinction and their dressmakers may possess the utmost facilities for constructing their costumes with the most approved Taste in the Highest and most Perfect Style of Fashion'. In 1850 there were nine other well-known fashion magazines selling and five others began soon after.

The patterns had been sold to dressmakers at an earlier date. Before the 1830s a Mrs Smith of London had sold full-size paper patterns at £1 the set. Her Paris partner, Madame Le Poulli, was resident there, so 'every novelty will be forwarded the moment they appear in the French capital'. A Mrs Hobson sold

cheaper patterns, 8s. for a set of four articles, whilst in 1831 Mr Reed in Blooms-
bury sold both men and women's patterns, with beautiful colour prints, at 8s. the
set. Besides selling these through booksellers Mr Reed, a tailor himself, had a
branch of his tailor's shop in Brooklyn, New York. The new idea of pattern,
drawing and magazine coming together was extremely popular and proved a
standard way of selling patterns till the Second World War when paper restrictions
hit firms like Weldons.

The nineteenth-century patterns were printed on tissue paper but more than
one pattern was printed on top of the other. The first set issued with *The World of
Fashion* had a dress, bonnet and cape on one large sheet of tissue. In 1873 Buttericks
of America opened offices in London. They posted coloured plates to tailors and
dressmakers all over the world. Their patterns were less complicated to follow
and soon their Regent Street shop had a staff of 30–40 assistants. They produced
and sold between 40–60 new designs each month priced from 3d. to 2s. each.

41   Gulliver and the Lilliputians. A late nineteenth century advertisement for Coats Cotton. Note
the trade mark, adopted in the early days when they were uncommon.

Shops began to open separate pattern departments, especially as the fabrics and trimmings would usually be bought there as well. The fashion magazines would carry advertisements for materials and for dress shops. By 1870 many of the well-known firms like Debenham and Freebody were sending out fashion books with engravings so that customers could order by post.

Sewing the clothes became easier when Mr Clark of Paisley produced a smooth cotton thread for sewing. He first made this in 1806, selling it in hanks and skeins as he had meant it for a spinning process. Ladies bought it for use, winding it in balls for their sewing, or persuading Mr Clark to wind it on a spool for an extra halfpenny—returnable deposit on the spool. Till this time thread had always been silk and very expensive. Mr Clark continued his new trade, he wound different thicknesses of thread for different cloths selling them in small reels ticketed with the details. At the same time a Mr Coats of the same town needed fine twists of yarn to make his fine shawls of silk as delicate as the imported Chinese ones. Soon sewing thread from Clark or Coats was on sale in every drapery shop. In 1850 John Mercer, a Lancashire man, discovered how to make cotton yarn silky, 'mercerised' cotton. Not only could it be used for cloth but a cheap, silky finished cotton thread, easy to use with sewing machines, was now available.

More and more the clothing factories and the little sewing firms began to make underwear, cheap maids' outfits, sets of clothes for workmen, heavy corduroys, etc. The sewing machine had made it possible for most women still to look a little different by having her garments made by herself or by a dressmaker if they were outer garments. The shops tried to meet this need for clothes that would fit and yet have a more professional finish.

Until the 'princess' style, with no waistline cut into its smooth fit, all dresses had had been made with separate bodices for ordinary wear. When the difficult-to-make styles of the middle and late nineteenth-century came in, it was not surprising that shops began to sell things like 'muslin bodices exceedingly useful to the country trade . . . the dresses can be completed for wearing at a few hours notices' (*World of Fashion*, 1830). Later some sold clothes, part made, for dressmakers to finish, or skirts completely finished with bodices ready for trimming and fitting.

In 1866 Jays of London were advertising a 'self-expanding bodice, recommended to ladies in case of sudden bereavement or any less painful emergency, when ready made and stylish dress is required at a moments notice'.

By 1900 Peter Robinson's 'un-made dresses' only required joining at the back.

Further reading.
London Life and the Great Exhibition of 1851. Longmans Then and There Series.
Yarwood: *English Costume from B.C. to 1967.*
Huggett: *Shops.*
Reader: *Life in Victorian England.*
Doncaster: *Changing Society in Victorian England 1850–1900.*
Aldburgham: *Shops and Shopping.*

10 Darker and Darker

In the middle of Victoria's reign, clothes by day, at least in a town, would seem strangely dark to our eyes. This was partly because of the darker, heavier clothes men now wore, and partly because of the mourning customs. In their dress the middle class could mourn more fully and expensively, and there were few families who did not have reason to go into mourning in these days of early (compared with ours) deaths and high child mortality. Two years of black was considered correct for a respectable widow. If there was a death in the family the whole family, children, servants, relatives on both sides were expected to go into mourning. In 1864 the death rate in London was 34 to the thousand people compared with 12 in 1964. It was not surprising that firms like Jay's could occupy three houses in Regent Street and call themselves 'the London General Mourning Warehouse'.

Such shops sold full outfits of mourning but at a large funeral the providing of the black gloves presented to each mourner was a sizeable order alone. The rules said 'Mothers for the mother in law or father in law of their married children should wear black for six weeks', whilst a widow had not only to trim her summer parasol with black crepe but could wear no ornaments but jet for the first year. After Queen Victoria set the example of staying in mourning after her husband died, many other widows retained their mourning for the rest of their lives. Even before this there was a comic sketch on the subject called 'The House of Mourning':

Lady: I wish, Sir, to look at some mourning.
Shopman: Certainly; by all means. A relict, I presume?
Lady: Yes; a widow, sir. A poor friend of mine who has lost her husband.
Shopman: Exactly so; for a deceased. How deep would you choose to go? Do you wish to be very poignant? We have the very latest novelties from the Continent. Here is one Ma'am, just imported, a widow's silk— watered, you perceive, to match the sentiment. It is called 'Inconsolable', and is very much in vogue . . . we have several new fabrics to meet the demand for fashionable tribulation. . . . Or if you would prefer velvet?
Lady: Is it proper, sir, to mourn in velvet?
And so it goes on.

One draper's shop even gave away free a book *Mourning Etiquette*, so that 'all trouble may be avoided in deciding the degree of mourning proper to be worn under various losses'.

Mourning could be bought ready made. It was popular with many firms for this reason, as the dressmaking and tailoring hands in their 'made to measure' workrooms could be kept occupied with this work when orders were slack.

Dark men's clothes were now taken for granted. Disraeli, the Prime Minister, had worn green velvet, —flashing rings, and bright slippers brought back from his travels, but little trace of this could be seen in the sombre clothes he wore in the House of Commons. The last of the great dandies had been the handsome Count d'Orsay. Any garment he wore became the fashion. Once he was caught in a rainstorm and bought a rough jacket from a sailor; the next day rough jackets were all the rage. He wore bright colours. One visitor describes him wearing a striped waistcoat 'of a tender shade, light pantaloons and a brilliantly coloured redingote worn wide open'. By 1890 the Queen's son, the Duke of Clarence, was 'a whale on collars and cuffs, possessing the most elaborate and varied assortment of neck wear that can be found anywhere in the Queen's dominions'. By then it was one of the few ways a well-dressed man could be different! For the poorer man the detachable collar, though much frowned on, was creeping in, false shirt fronts called 'dickies' could even be bought—a feature of the lower- and middle-class trade.

Only in his waistcoat did the Victorian middle-class man have a chance for display. In the 1840s one of them was made in 'rich crimson velvet embroidered on the front with bullion-edged silk flowers and twining tendrils': later they were

42 Widows weeds. Mourning clothes like these could be made from patterns selling at 2s. 6d. each in 1879. Notice the sombre scenery behind. An illustration in Sylvia's Home Journal.

43 Interior of the London Stock Exchange, 1847. Notice the top hats. This scene is early Victorian. As time passed so did the light coloured top coats and trousers, giving way to more sombre shades.

darker, but the fabric could still be rich or at least decorated by gold fobs and watch chains.

Evening dress for men was even more sombre. One visitor wrote in 1878: 'Englishmen wear the same dress at an evening party and at a funeral. Nor is this all, for many a host who entertains his friends at dinner has a butler behind his chair who is dressed precisely like himself.' Only in his sporting dress could a more dashing mode be chosen.

Meanwhile the new chemical dyes were widely used, as they were so much cheaper. A vivid emerald green dye lost popularity in the '60s when a young girl going to a dance in a dress of this dye was seriously ill. In London an artificial flowermaker died after working with artificial leaves dyed this green. A Berlin doctor said that 60 grains of arsenic powder could fall from a dress this colour in one night, enough to kill 30 people! Brilliant purples, pinks and blues continued to be popular, too popular a visiting writer thought. He described 'a violet bonnet, pink bows outside, sky blue strings and a green veil'.

Some people tired of these crude, brilliant colours and the artificial style of dress for women. Most of them believed with William Morris, one of the leaders of the back to nature movement, that 'no dress can be beautiful that is stiff, drapery is essential'. He set up workshops to dye fabrics in the softer, natural colours and produced beautiful wallpapers, furniture and hangings. Most of the writers and artists with these ideas were lucky in having outstandingly beautiful wives and daughters to wear them. It was a style also taken up by some Society women of the time.

65

44 On top of a horse bus. By 1865 darkness in dress has spread. Notice the man on the kerb: mufflers and collars were almost the symbols separating working class and office workers.

One, the Duchess of Rutland, has been described by her daughter as wearing these 'aesthetic' clothes (as they were called), 'with very high heeled pointed shoes with buckles, to increase her height, beautiful slim legs and ankles, a small waist drawn tightly into a silver buckled petersham belt, a creamy flimsy open necked shirt. . . . In London for outdoors there were face cloth clothes—greenish-greyish-bluish-fawnish—with tabs and smoked flat pearl buttons'. Liberty's was the new shop that first imported and then had made in England these delicate fabrics and softly printed materials.

William Morris himself wore a big grey cloak and a large-brimmed soft grey hat, comfortable tweeds and hand-knitted sturdy stockings. In 1890 he wrote a book called *News from Nowhere* about England in the 1960s, predicting soft, simple garments with fine leather belts and the most gorgeous clothes reserved for dustmen to show that lowly work is respected. Few working men ever saw Morris's clothes, but Oscar Wilde, the sophisticated playwright, also had ideas about simpler clothes and patronised the shop Liberty had opened. 'I hate the dreadful chimney-pot hat and shocking swallow-tail coat', said Wilde, little realising that today we imagine most Englishmen of his day dressed not in these clothes but in the deer-stalker hats and tweed trousers worn by Sherlock Holmes, a character in a book! A jacket called the 'dress lounge', our present dinner jacket, came in by the 1890s but this tail-less coat was modelled on the lounge jacket popular in the 1880s; our present type of suit jacket comes from this. In the 1880s it was already very popular, with pleats in the back, large pockets and often made of Harris tweed. It was favoured by the new writers like Bernard Shaw and his friends who were part of the new movement for getting out into the countryside for walking and cycling.

More and more 'health' and healthy activities became the fashion. Dr Jaeger, a

Professor of Zoology, believed that pure wool next to the skin was best. His type of underwear especially became famous. Only the richer people could follow the fashion completely; in any case it was reported in 1906 that the 'vast majority of gentlemen dispense with underwear altogether during the summer months'. A lady, told that wool next to her skin was necessary 'to absorb perspiration' complained in 1885: 'a gentlewoman rarely does anything to cause such an unpleasant thing'.

All the same Jaeger clothes flourished, Bernard Shaw bought a complete Jaeger outfit of brown knitted wool and another of grey. Women were so determined to get this new woollen underwear that 'ladies would drive up in their carriages . . . and carry off the precious bales without waiting for them to be wrapped up'.

45 A Navvy on the tramp, 1855. Notice the stout boots and neckerchief. The hat is very like the tarpaulin covered and water-resisting ones of sailors of the day.

46 Norfolk jacket and deerstalker, 1886. The jacket has a smart military style collar despite the tweed cloth. He wears good gaiters and tiny boots; the small feet were a fashion drawing idea—small feet were meant to mean upper class.

The fashionable world of Edward VII, Queen Alexandra and court beauties like Lily Langry and Mrs Keppel were little influenced by these styles. The bustles, the piled-up padded hair, the pearl dog-collars still remained with the spats, canes and heavy cloth of the men. What Morris did not realise in suggesting simple tweeds, corduroys, heavy boots, the uniform of the workmen of his day, was that these were thought of as the clothing of manual workers and so had little appeal to the working classes. Today, when wages have risen and many of these jobs have more status, these clothes have more appeal.

Further reading.
Lindsay and Washington: *A Portrait of Britain 1851–1951*.
Harrison and Royston: *Late Nineteenth Century Picture Source Book*.
Dulton: *The Victorian Home*.
Gernsheim: *Fashion and Reality*.

11 New Ways in Making and Selling

In the last years of the nineteenth century most people, especially women, still wore a surprising quantity of clothes, despite new Jaeger wool underwear. Nor were they easy to put on. 'There must have been something aristocratic about buttons in those days, for everything that could possibly button and unbutton was made to do so: buttons all down the front of one's nightgown, buttons on the sleeves, buttons on one's bodices and drawers, buttons everywhere.' The same writer—Gwen Raverat—described the clothes of a young girl of the day:

1   Thick, long legged, long-sleeved woollen combinations.
2   Over them, white cotton combinations, with plenty of buttons and frills.
3   Very serious, bony, grey stays, with suspenders.
4   Black woollen stockings.
5   White cotton drawers, with buttons and frills.
6   White cotton 'petticoat bodice' with embroidery, buttons and frills.
7   Rather short, white flannel, petticoat.
8   Long alpaca petticoat, with a flounce round the bottom.
9   Pink flannel blouse.
10 High, starched white collar, fastened with studs.
11 Navy blue tie.
12 Blue skirt, touching the ground, and fastened tightly to the blouse with a safety pin behind.
13 Leather belt, very tight.
14 High button boots.

Younger children going to school did not wear school uniform, certainly girls did not. The attempt to keep their clothes clean can be seen at both ends of the social scale, pinnies or pinafores were worn to school by poorer children (overall pinafores are still common in Germany and France today) whilst at Eton boys had taken to wearing dickies!

The same girl who listed the clothing explained how clothes were taken apart and made into new ones in her quite well-to-do home. As clothes continued their elaborate way, as far as women were concerned, this was not surprising. Ladies, even married ones, had ceased to wear caps indoors, but all kinds of flower and feather decorations became fashionable on clothes as well as hats. 'Some twenty to thirty million dead birds are imported into this country annually to supply the demands. When the wind blew, the heavy ornamented hats tore at the wearer's head, especially if they were skewered to mountains of false hair. The crinoline had gone much earlier, by the 1870s, but 'tiebacks' had become popular, the skirt tied back so that 'a fashionable lady walking along was barely able to move

47 A London telephone exchange in 1883. A number of jobs in offices etc., began to be filled by women even before 1914. Money of their own in their pockets gave women an independence that perhaps only factory girls had known before; money of their own to spend as they liked.

her feet six inches at a time'. The bustle developed, housemaids were said to borrow two or three of their mistresses' dusters to puff themselves out to the required shape when off duty.

Poorer people could not easily compete with the cloth and labour needed for such outfits, even if they had been practical for their everyday life. Nor could they cope with the intricate cut. Some men's clothes were now being manufactured both in Yorkshire, especially Leeds, and in London. Many of the immigrants from Eastern Europe at this time, especially Russia, were skilled in the tailoring trades and worked in or set up small workshops for ready-to-wear clothes. Women's clothes were more difficult. Apart from the cut, fashion changed more quickly and their complications made it more difficult to produce them in factories, although underwear was sold ready-made on a large scale.

An iron worker in Middlesbrough in Edwardian times earned about 19s. 6d. a week. At the most the family of three could afford 1s. a week for clothes, but few families were as small as this! Men needed clothes for their job, so the women did without. Long skirts covered cheap boots. The boots could be second-hand 'boiled boots', patched up and polished from the 'boiled boot shop'. Some women pawned their husband's clothes every week, as his were usually the best in the family: they were 'popped' on Monday for about 3s. 6d. and taken out again on Saturday for 4s. More respectable families tried cutting down old adult's clothes for the children and passing on the children's clothes down the family from child to child.

Most families tried to keep respectable, but if father drank heavily or was sick, or the mother deserted or widowed, the most extraordinary clothes might be worn by children. Charlie Chaplin's mother sent his brother Sidney to school in 'a coat from her old velvet jacket. It had red and black striped sleeves, pleated at the shoulder . . . the coat and a pair of mother's cut down high heeled shoes got him into many a fight at school'. Charlie 'with a pair of Mother's red tights cut down for stockings was called "Sir Francis Drake".'

Even the Salvation Army's women officers found it hard to pay £1 for their uniform 'Princess' robes and black straw bonnets with missile resistant brims, and a guinea for the Captain's outfit, from the clothing workshop which the Army had set up for itself. A cheap wool cloth, shoddy, made largely from ground up woollen rags, had long since provided a cheaper wool fabric, whilst Australian sheep farms were now providing cheaper new wool. But a cheaper way of making clothes had to be worked out.

Some large stores had already reduced prices by buying on a large scale. In 1886 Lewis's of Liverpool were selling a quarter of a million hats a year at 3s. 9d. not their normal 6s. 6d. The Hat and Cap Traders Association threatened to cut off their supplies but were told, 'Lewis's sell more hats in a week than most middle-men can buy in a month, and the manufacturer knows too well who are the best customers to allow themselves to be dictated to in that manner.' Direct buying from maker to store had begun.

In large towns and London, firms like Moss Brothers were selling second-hand or misfit trousers from 6s. 6d. to 10s. 6d. in 1900, overcoats for 12s. 6d. and suits for 35s.–45s., but these prices were too high for general buyers, as their hire prices were. Many buyers still resorted to the tallyman and his 'tick' as credit was called, or if they were lucky, a jumble sale.

An ironworker in Scotland said, 'the tallyman provided all the wearing apparel at our home and in every home in Cowie Square. I suppose the good customers had to make up for the bad ones, but the tallyman got his money weekly at our door for years. We never grew rich enough to buy for ready money. Craigneuk was so completely working class that my mother couldn't hope for real bargains in wearing apparel. There were no prosperous folk to do the needful at the jumble sale.'

The coming of war in 1914 spread the growth of the clothing industry. About three quarters of a million British died in battle, countless more passed through the

48 Girls playing hockey, 1893. Even with the hats this was far more sensible than some of the ladies' sporting outfits of the time: tennis in embroidered velvet 'tennis aprons' and so on.

49 Elizabethan fashions popular in 1891. Not only were fancy dress balls popular in 'Society' (a new word that had come in to describe the rich who surrounded Edward VII and his friends) but many historical styles came in as novelties.

50 'Found.' This countryman was painted in the 1850's, but smock and leggings were still standard working wear in many country areas before the 1914 war.

51 'The Health of the Bride, 1889.' This picture of a working class wedding with sailor best man shows how far changes in manufacture had improved ordinary people's clothes. At a wedding they are, of course, all wearing their best.

country's armed forces. All had to be equipped and clothed. Millions of garments were needed in fairly standardised sizes and an almost completely standard style. The better tailoring workshops already had not only power machines for hems and a machine which sewed on buttons and made button holes, but also the power sewing and bulk cutting-out machines. The Eastman cutter, from America, like most of these sewing inventions, provided a small, powered hand-cutter better suited to small workshops. The Hoffman presser could also be used instead of the endless heating of pressing irons, the tailor's 'goose'.

It was simpler to have workers in the factory, it was easier to have each worker make part of a garment rather than the whole. After the war these workshops remained: some went bankrupt, others turned to civilian work. Sizing was more standardised and more and more men bought ready-made suits for work, especially when large stores like Pontings of London advertised in the daily papers for mail orders, or sent out catalogues. Stores were more common. An outing to the shops was a treat when radio and films were only just beginning and entertainments were in short supply. The car and bus brought many country people to the shops each weekend. Ready-to-wear clothes available on hangers, displayed on models, made a direct appeal to the buyer that cloth had never had.

Women's clothing changed more slowly but the war had simplified styles and cut down on the quantities of material needed. Besides the usual drapery-store ready-mades, produced in the slack season, some clothing factories even before the war were making children's clothes, women's blouses, skirts and coat frocks. Factory tailors with spare space after the war turned to women's tailoring. The new rayon material proved ideal for dress manufacture. It was cheaper in price

52 *Shopman:* 'Excuse me, Madam, but am I not right in presuming you come from the Toy Department?' *Lady:* 'Certainly. Why?' *Shopman:* 'Would you very kindly direct me to it? I'm one of the Assistants there and I've lost my way.'

Cartoon about a large store, 1911. Notice the huge muff, fur scarf and hat, the skirt and over-skirt as well. The assistant wears striped trousers and long coat.

1022-20

than silk but at the same time was better adapted for making up into fashionable dresses. Attractive and fashionable rayon dresses encouraged customers to prefer ready-made clothes.

The new rayon also allowed girls to wear rayon imitation silk stockings. War work had freed many younger women in a way unknown before. They had money to spend, and this was a more valuable equality than anything that could be obtained by the clamour for women's rights. Short skirts and 'young' fashion popularised the flesh-coloured stockings, the cloche or head hugging hat and the short-haired shingle. Before the war Gwen Raverat begrudged paying 10s. for a pair of silk stockings: by 1939 Woolworths were selling fine rayon stockings at 1s. per pair, 6d. a stocking bought singly.

The new short skirt of skimpy cut made home dressmaking possible for the amateur with or without a sewing machine. The cost in cloth was small. Even smart well-to-do American girls like Cornelia Otis Skinner, daughter of a rich acting family and able to afford a visit to Europe, made her own frocks.

There was no reason why a pretty girl in such a frock with her uniform shingled head should not be 'classless' in looks, in a way never known before. Men's wear, too, was beginning to change in this direction. A romantic novelist of the day described how the heroine looked at the debonair, well-tailored shape of the young man coming down the road . . . and then realised it was the boy from next door.

Further reading.
Edwardian England. Longman Then and There Series.
Suffragettes and the Votes for Women. Longman Then and There series.
Unstead: *Book IV.* Century of Change.
Sitwell: *Victorian Narrative Painting.*

53 Film star in short skirts. Clara Bow in *It*. Styles like these, and even shorter skirts, were copied all over the world. They were imitated more widely and faster than ever before because even poor people went to the cinema or saw magazine pictures.

12 Fashion for All

As long ago as 1664 an English scientist named Hooke said 'there might be found a way to make an artificial composition much resembling . . . the substance out of which the silkworm draws his clew' (thread)? In 1745 a Frenchman said, 'Silk is only liquid gum'. In 1878 Joseph Swan experimenting to make a filament for an electric bulb made a fine thread of artificial material. It was not till the twentieth century that two English chemists made a viscose liquid, the basis of rayon, and two others discovered how to strengthen it for thread. Courtaulds, the textile firm, took it up and by 1900 8,000 tons of rayon thread were manufactured. The rayon, mostly made from wood, marks the beginning of our present age of 'manufactured fibres'.

Once large-scale production has begun, man-made fabrics can be produced cheaply and to the exact thickness or thinness asked for by the customer. They take colours easily, usually with little or no bleaching before dyeing. Rayon was the great artificial material of the period between the wars.

Nylon was discovered by an American, W. H. Carothers, when he was trying to make artificial rubber. Nylon was an artificial fibre made from coal, air, water and some vegetable oils, it was strong but could be made to stretch like elastic. In January 1940, the first nylon fibre was ready for delivery to American mills for stockings and fabrics. When America joined the war in 1941 the new 'silk' was found ideal for parachutes, tyres, resistant fabrics. A few Englishwomen knew of the magic 'non-ladder' (compared with silk and rayon) stockings made of nylon they had got perhaps as gifts from Americans; but it was not until two years after the Second World War that nylon was made on a large scale commercially in England.

The 1939–45 war not only called for millions of yards of cloth and countless uniforms as the previous World War had done; it also meant a great call for new materials. Britain discovered Terylene during the war. Like nylon it was rot- and moth-proof, easily washed and dried. It could in fact be drip-dried to need no ironing. The two materials made clean shirts and underwear possible in a way even the rich had not known in earlier years. In the next 20 years makers of the traditional fabrics, wool and cotton, were to produce some of these qualities in their materials. Terylene itself was not put on the market till 1950, because the Government had declared it an Official Secret during the war.

Orlon, a synthetic material, has been introduced to take the place of wool, still the softest, warmest and longest-wearing of all natural fibres. A vast new market was open in the clothing industry for these products.

After the war the factory change to civilian garments was quicker than it had been after the first World War. The government issued each member of the forces with a demobilisation or 'demob' suit: a hat, a shirt with two collars, cuff links and studs, two pairs of socks and one of shoes, as well as a 14-day ration card, were provided. Clothes were still rationed as they had been throughout the war, but women fell heavily for the 'New Look' brought in by Christian Dior in Paris after the war. But it was a 'New Look severely modified for Liverpool Street (a London railway station famous for commuter office workers) in the rush hour . . . for a mass sale ladies' garment industry' says a writer on those days.

Before the war large stores like Selfridges had used skilful display to encourage middle-class women to take more interest in ready-made clothes. There were more branded names now, that buyers knew could be relied on for good fit and cut. Most women lived far away from London, however, and even when shops like C. and A. Modes brought prices down by concentrating on inexpensive clothing this only happened in their few branches in the large towns. But in the late 1920s one chain of stores based especially in the Northern counties entered into the inexpensive clothes field for both men and women.

Marks and Spencer began with a 'penny bazaar' in Leeds in 1884. As it grew two definite ideas stayed from those days—clear prices and customers choosing their own purchases (a novel idea for clothes in the days of plentiful shop assistants). In 1927, after one of the chiefs had returned from America the stores switched to nothing over 5s. In two or three years over 70 per cent of the goods they usually sold were no longer on their counters, but more and more clothing goods that sold at under 5s. (e.g. jumpers at 1s. 11d.). By 1939 they had 234 branch stores which enabled them to buy, for example, huge orders of grey cloth and get it made up to their standards. Clothing was to be of as good a quality as the price would allow and the firm laid rules about the standards they expected from their cloth.

When the war came people were restricted to 66 clothing coupons a year, later only half this number. The Government, in its researches before bringing in

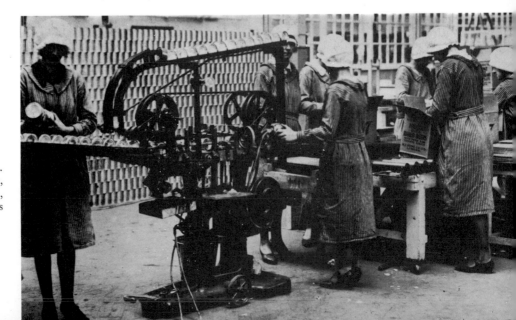

54 Heinz factory girls, 1929. Notice the protective clothing, easily washable cotton. Nylon, even more easily cleaned, is used generally today.

55 Privates of World War II. Notice the 'battle dress' type uniform, easy to take off, put on and work in. Even some of the officers have adopted it. The General's clothes are reminiscent of World War I with the exaggerated riding breeches. At the back stands an American officer. The simpler style was easier for mass-production and for a reasonable fit for varied shapes.

coupons, had discovered just how shoddy and short-lived much cheap clothing was. The people who bought it, the poor, were the ones who had fewest stocks to fall back on as rationing came in. In order to make sure that decent clothes sold at reasonable prices a 'Utility' clothing scheme was introduced by the Government. Numbers of pleats and so on were restricted to save cloth but at least the Utility mark made sure that the garment was of a reasonable standard. To attract the customer more, these clothes were sold without the one third of its total price purchase tax, which was the minimum tax paid on other clothes.

The Government laid down cloth standards and the measurement of different sizes. Besides sizing the war brought good design into cheap clothes. To mass produce the lines had to be well and simply cut in women's as well as men's clothes. To encourage people to buy 'utility' top designers were asked to adapt their ideas for clothes to be made in thousands, not for the individual customer.

In 1949 when clothes rationing ended Marks and Spencers decided that fashion clothing was going to be one of their main lines. War had got rid of the 5s. top price. Now they decided to concentrate on good, hard-wearing materials and good styling. When the 'Utility' restriction went in 1952 they were able to upgrade still more.

The new synthetics or artificial fibres of the '50s were seized upon by stores such as Marks and Spencers. They had the good wearing qualities their customers demanded, they could often be standardised more easily: the fact that they were produced in large quantities by large firms made bulk buying much easier. Processes with new machinery like that for knitted goods and wool jersey were quick to expand and sweaters and jerseywear became a great speciality. They used their own brand name, whatever the supplier. It came to have the same reputation for dependability that the expensive brand names had created before the war. This was especially so of underwear. When nylon was comparatively new the firm used it to make underwear, not perhaps the cheapest available, but in lavish, delicate styles previously reserved only for high fashion and the rich. Thick corded dressing gowns gave way to negligees, the dressing gowns themselves had been a novelty at first in a shop specialising in cheap clothes.

As one of their suppliers said of Marks and Spencers, 'They are not a charitable institution', but the new methods made good profits for their shareholders and encouraged many other firms to adopt similar clothing ideas. By expecting to 'get a Rolls Royce at a Ford's prices', by paying suppliers on the dot, the stores were able to attract a new class of customer. Duchesses in newspaper interviews said they shopped there, large numbers of people paid for their clothes by cheque.

Mail-order firms were also expanding, their catalogues became fatter and their turnover increased as they found a new public. Usually they had found customers through 'agents' who collected week by week in return for a commission. This 'club' idea continued but more people began to buy their clothes through the catalogue advertisements, often paying the price in ready money and not weekly dues, frequently using the catalogue only for their family and its needs. The shopper in the remote country district found these large, entirely mail order firms provided more information and stock than the mail order booklets of the ordinary stores. Top designers were persuaded to either design, or oversee, the choice of the fashion goods. Well known branded names agreed to sell their garments through the catalogue pages and even to design a special range to be sold only in this way.

Magazines also provided a way not only for finding out about clothes and the latest new materials but also in providing them for their readers themselves.

56 Girls in the ATS. The aim for women's uniforms seemed to be to keep as near as possible to male uniform—except for the WREN who not only had the smart navy and white but was allowed to wear black silk stockings if available.

57 A provincial Marks and Spencers, 1939. Notice the prices in the window.

Woman magazine sold in one year over a million pounds worth of cut-out garments which were woven, printed and cut out exclusively for the magazine. In 1937, the first cut-out offer had been an artificial satin nightie at 4s. 11d., an offer which sold a few thousands: the figures after the war rose to 100,000 orders for a jersey frock at two guineas. In 1962 one week's offer produced 107,746 orders for the garment, a suit in double jersey wool. The cost of the goods came to £269,853.

Clothes were simpler and so much cheaper ready-made. The novelty of buying new, clean firsthand clothes was forgotten as it was accepted that all classes could do so. The new washing machines, better soap powders and detergents and cheap Coin-op dry cleaners kept them in good condition. Pale colours were normal town wear. Best suits might still be tailor made to fit but most clothes that went with them would be bought from one or other of the large stores and firms.

Men, perhaps traditionally the dandies, were the first to break out. Young men now earned high wages, they wanted something less uniform before National Service put them into uniform. The 'zoot suit' appeared, made to the customer's own ideas by the local tailor: the young upper class male might try a longer skirted coat and narrow trousered Regency look for his outfit. (Regency is the style of clothing worn about the time of Waterloo.) Compared with many of these new styles for men the women's 'New Look' was almost a uniform.

Younger girls tried to look different from their elders. A new, simple suit, straight skirt and almost cardigan type jacket had been designed by a famous French designer of the 1920s and '30s, Madame Chanel. Balenciaga, perhaps the greatest of the Paris designers, had brought in the simplest of all frocks, the shift. This was another idea that looked back to the '20s. These were elegant clothes for the elegant older woman.

The tweed sports jacket and grey flannels men had worn as casual wear at the weekends before the war became normal working wear for many after it. Casual and sports clothes had always had a dashing appeal. The admired sections of the armed forces in World War II: the pilots, the Desert Rats of the Eighth Army, had been famous for casual easy-to-wear clothes they adapted from their uniform. In days of servant shortage civilian clothes like these were easy to look after. Women also found the stiff pre-war suits uncomfortable after the slacks, sweaters and overalls they had worn on active service and in the wartime factories. Worse still, they seemed curiously ageing in their stiffness. Everyday styles for both men and women became more casual.

In the home women had more and more labour-saving machines. Hours in the factory and office were shorter. In time a weekend that included a full Saturday and Sunday free became normal in most jobs. More people had time to take up sports, they needed the clothes for this. Many more, maybe, took up no new sport but saw the need for different, more easily worn clothes for relaxing in.

The large stores were especially fitted to meet the need. The new leisure clothes were often bought as 'separates': chunky sweater and casual slacks for both men and women. Sizing was, therefore, easier and more adaptable. Foreign holidays made more people conscious of other modes from anoraks to bikinis.

By the 1960s very short skirts were being worn by the young, with the Russian boot (so popular in 1924) returning with the short skirts and even shorter mini-skirts. This style, somewhat chilly for our Northern climate, was helped out by trousers becoming more and more accepted for every kind of wear. Leather and suede, originally confined to coats, were used for skirts and frocks.

The new style clothes, made at first for a small public, spread. As they spread, once more the wholesalers and clothing manufacturers joined the movement. The 'Carnaby Street' look came in, Mary Quant designed collections for both the

58 Utility Mark. The 'Utility Mark' stamped or labelled on all clothes made to suit the Government's utility requirements.

59 New Look frocks. These were styles in Vogue, April 1949, when the New Look had become accepted.

British market and America, Biba and similar 'instant fashion' shops sent out mail-order catalogues. Large numbers of small, specialist dress shops opened. They tried to give customers a small choice of clothes, specially chosen to represent the shops 'style'. The smallness and personal service, the pre-selection by the shop of garments from the huge range turned out today appealed to young and often rather unsure customers more than the large impersonal store. Records were often played, coffee bars sometimes part of the shop. Many ceased to be merely 'boutiques' and became a popular meeting-place for young people with money to spend, especially in the smaller provincial towns. The large stores were forced to do the same, either with small 'shop in a shop' areas displaying all the styles of one manufacturer or for one age range, or seeking the coffee bar-boutique atmosphere on a larger scale like 'Miss Selfridge' (Selfridges) or the 'Way In' (Harrods) in London.

One of the selling points of the 'Way In' as opposed to 'Miss Selfridge' is that

60 A 1962 wedding dress. Mr George Woodcock, then General Secretary of the TUC, with his daughter Vilja. Many weddings now have not only the long white dress but 'morning dress' for the men. More and more the type of occasion, rather than social background, decides the clothes to be worn.

many of the clothes are designed to be worn by either sex—'Unisex' clothes. So far the idea is that girls wear trousers: except for dressing gown caftans and night shirts for men there had been little sign of 'unisex' skirts. This may be a fashion to come, certainly fabrics and materials will continue to change in the Space Age. In the past, although everybody wore clothes for protection, warmth, attraction, uniform or prestige, only the very few were able to have new, well-fitting fashionable clothes. In Britain today it is assumed clothes and fashion go together, on sale to all.

Further reading.
Derry and Jarman: *The Making of Modern Britain.*
Bayne-Jardine: *World War Two.*
Present day newspapers and magazines.

13 Children's Clothes

Children, for very many years, were dressed as small editions of their parents, whether they worked by their side in the fields or were clad in the latest fashion of the day. In the Middle Ages the boys wore a loose gown almost to the ankles: for more practical wear it would be shorter, with a slit at the front from the hem to give more freedom of movement. Whereas adults always wore a belt, children's gowns were not necessarily belted: under the gown loose-fitting drawers were tied round the boy's waist.

A boy would wear a hood attached to a cape round his shoulders. The cape kept the hood in place on his head. When the hood was pushed back it would hang down behind. The point at the back of the hood became longer until it was a hanging tail called a liripipe. This headdress is so warm and protects the neck and head so well that a version of it has been worn by soldiers in most wars since. The modern version, with no liripipe to make it gay, is worn today and called a balaclava after the battle of the Crimean War of Queen Victoria's day.

Little girls wore long plain gowns or kirtles, which they fastened at the back like their mothers, with lacing from the neck to the waist. They were expected to wear a coif, a plain fitting linen bonnet on their head, often with a veil draped over. They seem also, however, to have been allowed to go bareheaded, as can be seen in the many pictures of the children of ordinary people. Noble and royal children had clothes of great richness. When in 1377 Isabella of Valois, at the age of nine, married Richard II, King of England, she had a surcoat of red velvet embossed

61 Two small boys. Both boys wear long gowns with hoods that can be pulled over their heads.

62   Prince Frederick of Urbino. This little Italian prince is swaddled tightly in long bands of cloth. The covering is of scarlet silk, heavy with pure gold embroidery.

with birds of a goldsmith's work, perched on branches woven in pearls and emeralds; the border of the gown was of ermine. When Dante, the Italian poet, first saw Beatrice, the girl whom he loved all his life, she was not ten years old. She also wore red. 'She appeared before me dressed in a most noble colour, a humble and honest dark red, dressed and adorned in such a fashion as was befitting her very young age.'

Tiny babies were swaddled as they had always been; swaddling bands of linen or wool bound the baby from neck to foot, his biggin (coif) covered most of the rest. Babies were swaddled like this until the eighteenth century and even later. The infants must have got extremely sodden but this does not seem to have deterred their mothers; not till safety pins became cheap and easy to obtain did the habit die out completely. The swaddling bands were often put over a simple shirt, so that from time to time the bands could be taken off and the baby allowed to kick. In a Tudor book the mother and nurse talk together:

'Unswaddle him', the mother says, 'undoe his swaddling bands . . . wash him before me. . . . Pull off his shirt, thou art pretty and fat my little darling. . . . Now swaddle him again. But first put on his biggin and his little band (collar) with an edge, where is his little petticote? Give him his cote of changeable (shot) taffata and his sattin sleeves: Where is his bibbe? . . .'

An Italian painting shows the beautiful christening and presentation robes all tightly swaddled round the little prince who wears them. The Tudor book that describes the dressing of the baby also describes a schoolboy dressing in the same frenzied haste as a schoolboy today. He does, however, have the maid, Margaret, to help him.

85

63 Tudor children. Notice how the tiny child is dressed almost as stiffly as the adult. How are the girls distinguished from the boy?

Margaret: 'Ho, Frauncis, rise and get you to school: you shall be beaten, for it is past seven: make yourself ready quickly . . .'

Francis: 'Margarite, geeve me my hosen: hurry I pray you. Where is my doublet? Bryng my garters and my shooes . . .'

Margaret: 'Take first a clean shirt for yours is fowle.'

Francis: 'Make haste then, for I do tarry too long.'

Margaret: 'It is moyst (damp) yet, tarry a little that I may drie it by the fire.'

Francis: 'Where have you laid my girdle and my inckhorne? Where is my gyrkin (jerkin) of Spanish leather of Bouffe? Where be my socks of linen . . . my cap, my hat, my coate, my kaipe (cape or short cloak), my gowne, my gloves, my mittayns (mittens), my slippers . . . where is all my gear? I have nothing ready: I will tell my father.'

Till the age of about six this boy would have worn a gown. Then he was 'breeched'—put into doublet and hose. (The wearing of gowns or frocks continued in many families until late Victorian times.)

86

In the eighteenth century 'petticoats' as they were called were common for young boys, both rich and poor. Samuel Crompton, the inventor of the spinning mule, writes about the work he did in the home when he was young:

> The cotton wool was put into a deep brown tub with a strong lye of soap and suds. My mother then tucked my petticoats about my waist and put me in the tub to tread upon the cotton at the bottom . . . the tub became so full that a chair was placed beside it and I held on by the back.

Lady Anne North described how a boy of six was breeched in 1679:

> You cannot believe the great concerne that was in the whole family . . . the day the taylor was to help dress little Frank in his breeches in order . . . never had any bride that was to be drest upon her wedding night more hands about her. . . . They are very fitt, everything, and he looks taller and prettyer than in his coats (petticoats).

Swords were carried by small boys till about the middle of the seventeenth century. They dressed so like their elders that in 1699 the Earl of Bristol paid £2 3s. for a periwig for his son who was not yet eight. Little girls of three were put into whalebone bodices.

Children were dressed in strong colours. Princess Elizabeth, the five-year-old daughter of James I, wore warm purple serge and brown Spanish frieze in winter. She also had gowns of yellow satin, of figured velvet black upon red, of white satin upon carnation, of Spanish taffetas trimmed with plush, of orange and green or blue crepe with metal fringes round the neck. Seven years later when her brother died she was 12. Her mourning dress was of black satin, brocaded with silver flowers. As one writer, Doris Langley Moore, says:

> Not a discomfort fashion could contrive but was promptly reproduced on a smaller scale for the nursery—the starched ruff, the buckram corset, swelling breeches stuffed with bombast, farthingales, hoopes, plumed head-dresses,

64 The Great Exhibition, 1851. A confrontation between the social classes on a 'shilling' day. The smocks, trousers and knee-boots of the labourer and his son contrast with the impractical clothes of the ladies. The differing headgear of the workmen show their trades.

these and a thousand other modish inventions served in their time to declare in the plainest manner the class to which a child's parents belonged or aspired.

At about the end of the eighteenth century a new fashion for boys appeared, a fashion that was taken up by men—trousers. Sailors and countrymen had worn trousers, but breeches were the normal wear of a gentleman. First the 'trowsers' were worn in the period between the frock and sash of babyhood and the breeches which had turned little boys at once into men. When trousers were tight fitting they were called pantaloons: Beau Brummell wore these and gave the seal of elegance to the new fashion. Although boys wore them with their waistcoats and coats, small boys often wore trousers buttoned onto and over the jacket. A fond mother described the suit her little boy of four wore when he was 'breeched' in this new way in 1790:

> Dear Frederick was breeched . . . the jacket and trousers were of cloth, the latter being buttoned over the jacket . . . underwaist-coats and drawers were not then worn, so I had the linings of the trousers made separate which ensured proper cleanliness.

Little girls were also slowly getting a style of dress of their own. Instead of wearing a miniature version of her mothers, except that it was usually in two parts and fastened down the back instead of being a 'round' gown, young girls now wore the low necked frocks of linen or cotton like those they had worn as babies. They were in pale colours, generally white, with coloured sashes. By the 1780s girls in their late teens were wearing this simple style; 'the white dresses are certainly the prettiest at your age', wrote a mother to her fifteen year old daughter who had been sent abroad to be educated at a French convent school. As the muslin became finer, slips of different colours could be worn underneath. (A fashion so attractive, and so obviously expensive in days when laundering cost so much, would not be long left to children. By the middle of the Napoleonic wars it had become the favourite adult style for young women.)

Under these frocks and slips girls wore white trousers. The first aim of this garment was to cover the ankles. They were often 'shams' that tied on at the knee: the expensive materials used for some of these knee-to-ankle trouser lengths proves that they were not used particularly for economy. This style meant that skirts could be shorter for girls and pictures are found of skirts well off the floor from about 1815 onwards. Drawings of children in the cotton mills of a little later show the girls in ragged skirts well above the ankles, and the bare feet common on the slippery factory floors. Young factory boys wore trousers, again often ragged and ending well above the ankle.

Further reading.
See end of Chapter 14.

14 Young Gentlemen and Ladies

But it is not until the 1860s that we begin to find fashions for the adolescent. Whilst the great fashion houses that catered for the rich had only thought of adult fashion, the new middle-class magazines offered patterns to the dressmaker for the whole family. A few magazines even began to cater for younger people. Although many fashion magazines show crinolines for children, photographs of them in their own clothes normally show full skirts, even lacy stiff petticoats, but seldom hoops. To negotiate the swaying crinoline hoops round the rather overcrowed mid-Victorian house without too much breaking of china and knickknacks must have been quite difficult for an adult: perhaps hoops were not altogether a success for young girls still likely to run about, however strict their training.

The Victorian girl and very young boy both wore pinafores over their clothes, as many French children still do today. From the piece of material tied round the neck, with perhaps holes for the arms that had been standard nursery wear in Regency days, the Victorians developed a range of more covering pinafores, some like little frocks, some in the same material as the frock. Sometimes the pinafore could even be worn on its own. *Cassell's Household Guide*, of about 1870, states that the holland pinafore may be worn over winter frocks and alone in the summer.

Queen Victoria's children set the fashion for tartans. 'The costume worn by the Prince of Wales, when at Balmoral, has set the fashion of adopting the complete highland costume', says the *Lady's Newspaper* of 1852. When the next generation, the Prince of Wales's two sons, were put into sailor suits the *Lady's World* of 1887 said, 'these suits are now selling in thousands'.

These fashions spread throughout the Continent, especially as Queen Victoria's daughters married into the various Royal families of Europe, frequently taking with them if not the English nanny or governess, then at least the English taste in children's clothes. Even today the sailor suit is frequently worn at first Communion services by small boys in Spain and France, and expensive babywear shops are often called 'The English Baby'.

Printed cottons with sprig patterns had been popular for children's dresses. Silk had also been used, especially in the middle of the century, if the parents were wealthy, but wool, whether tartan patterned or otherwise, seems to have stayed the warm favourite. Although in the early twentieth century Lady Diana Cooper's mother was considered rather unusual to dress her daughter in black and, again in the 1950s, black was regarded as daring for small children, the Victorians of the 1840–80s thought otherwise.

Black coats and jackets were not only suitable for girls, and certainly did not show the dirt, they were also useful as mourning in days when small children wore

mourning at least as heavy as adults. By the end of the century the new open air fashions of their parents meant that tweeds were popular for children as well as adults. The two-piece suit, the 'English' tailor-made (produced for women by the French designer Doucet, copying the idea Charles Worth originated for the Empress Eugenie), was adapted by mothers for their daughters and became almost a uniform for girls.

The uniform that was adopted by some of the girls' schools at the beginning of the twentieth century was aimed not so much at producing an attractive, becoming means of identifying the pupils of a school, but at discouraging an interest in dress. The drill and gymnastics clothes gradually developed into a kind of uniform for the girls. A North London Collegiate schoolgirl of 1893 states:

> On special calisthenic days the girls are encouraged to wear a regular gymnastic dress of dark blue flannel, serge or other woollen material, with a light blue sash for the sake of uniformity, over which a skirt can be buttoned on at the waist and removed as they enter the gymnasium.

Boys' schools copied as much as possible the clothing of the 'top' public schools. 'Eton jackets' were popular with striped trousers.

The Great War led to an easing in the stiffness of not only the clothing of adults but that of children also. Liberty silk, edged with shantung collars and with cuffs faggotted into place, light lawns from the same source and printed with similar patterns, usually heavily smocked, were still regarded as the kind of little girls' clothes that distinguished a well-to-do child in her summer clothes from a girl in her equally pretty 'Miss Muffet' sprigged cotton at 6½d. a yard. With small boys the distinction was often between the boy who wore a white or grey shirt, collar, tie and pullover with his grey shorts, and the one who wore the wool jersey with or without the wool tie sold with it. Caps were replacing hats not only for school but for everyday wear, though many boys wore caps only at school, as part of the uniform, and seldom elsewhere: the same was to happen to girls' hats after the Second World War.

The more expensive schools slowly found a new uniform for boys. The change from short trousers to long marked the division between child and boy or young man. Wearing the blazer of the school games teams was usually the privilege of the senior boys of the school. This garment, however, had all the advantages of the sports jacket, the approved casual wear for men of the inter-war years, and yet it was possible to make it an identifiable school garment. The many pockets made it possible to use one of them for a school crest or badge of authority. Lace and braid could be added, as appropriate to designate the gods of the school from the Head Boy and Captains downwards. The blazer was reasonably cheap, and

65 Children's compromise in the 1860s. Miss Georgina Batsford models the full-skirted, but hoopless type of dress which was the accepted practical wear for energetic young ladies. Note the mittens she wears to complete her outfit.

if this fact proved in some cases to be a disadvantage, colour could be used to make it more uncommon, identifiable and expensive. The story is still told in one school of the headmaster who, discarding Eton jackets for the new blazers, found that the colour which at that time cost the most and faded the most was purple. This colour has remained that of the school blazer in question, though the reason is no longer valid as a result of modern methods of dyeing.

Girls' schools too (in days when cricket was still the second summer game for most girls' secondary schools) found the blazer ideal. The standard winter wear for schoolgirls between the wars was the 'gymslip'—now no longer used for gym but still retaining its title. After the last war the gymslip fell out of favour and was replaced by a skirt, still with the same blouse and tie that had been a feminine copy of her brothers' school wear in 1914.

The 1944 Education Act divided up the old elementary schools that had previously educated most children until the age of 14. The Junior school continued the tradition of the elementary school as far as clothes were concerned, and uniform is seldom worn. The new Senior schools, however—Secondary Modern, Comprehensive, Bilateral, etc.—usually chose to wear uniform as did the Grammar and Public schools. The uniform was now useful in providing a common type

66   Children in Lambeth in the 1890s.

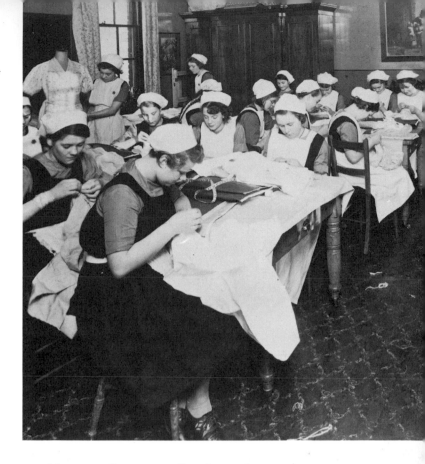

67 Blue Coat School needlework class, 1936. While learning to make clothes, these girls wear the typical 'gymslip' uniform adopted for every-day use.

of clothing for all pupils whatever their parents' income. It was usually planned on the lines of the local old-established Senior school, as the new schools wished to stress that they were comparable, unlike the old elementary or Board school. Not until the end of the 1950s did many schools begin to query their choice of uniform. Girls' schools have made perhaps the most radical changes but many people still doubt if the new fabrics and styles have the wearing qualities of the old. In some cases the collar, tie and even the boater of some girls' schools are regarded as a kind of charming old-fashioned costume that gives the schools a certain air. Certainly the girls' shirt and tie and the boys' blazer are very different from the clothes worn by their owners out of school.

The Second World War, with shortages of material and coupons, 'froze' fashions for young people not only for the war years but for some time after. Trousers had been worn by women and were now fairly common for girls as casual wear, the short jacket called the Eisenhower jacket and the cotton proofed windbreaker of the American forces was adopted for the same sort of wear. New materials were used, but as with their parents in the years just after the war there was little real change in fashion. Marks and Spencer and the large stores were producing good quality children's clothing at reasonable prices for all. Labour was scarce and help in the house hard to find. Many mothers worked full time, and both middle and working class children's clothes needed to be easy to keep clean, easy to put on and off and tough in wear. Even the clothes of the Royal children were not able to change this trend. As time passed and photographs were taken of them on less formal occasions they, too, were seen to be wearing the easier, simple clothes of the time.

It was the adolescents or 'teenagers' (as they were now called) who started the change. For the first time they had jobs and money: quite a lot of money, as even apprentices were now paid some wages as a result of full employment. Many young unskilled workers were paid at the same rate as older men doing the same job. They could dress themselves well; now it was often the boy at school who copied them. Far from teenage fashions following those of their parents the reverse happened. Now they could choose for themselves they experimented with what seemed like exotic and eccentric cuts and colours. Older men began to follow part of this new young look. They might not buy their trousers from John Stephen of Carnaby Street though some did, but they expected their tailor or shop to provide something similar. Television made normal what had seemed extraordinary. Royal lords and middle-aged dukes were seen on it wearing polo-necked shirts. To be young, fashion had to be more and more unusual: leather, suede, the new plastics were all used. For most teenage boys the bulk of these clothes were never worn to the extent that blue-jeans were. The other clothes were fine for casual wear, the jeans were useful for that but also for wearing to work instead of overalls. Girls wore them and the 'Western' look, harking back to cowboy days, was even more noticeable when boots became fashionable.

Young girls were the first to wear boots with their short mini-skirts. Whilst the most 'way-out gear' was never widely fashionable, the new rich teenage public could pay for magazines like *Honey, Petticoat* and *19*, when new magazines for older women sometimes failed. In turn, the mini-skirt and the 'maxi' coat, the sari drape and the Indian forehead band, the fun fur and the 'Victorian' look have had their followers. In the central areas of London young children followed the fashion with their own 'boutiques' with names like 'Kids in Gear'.

Certainly clothes for young people have become more comfortable than ever before. It seems unlikely that they will ever again return to small copies of their parents' styles, but more than likely that adults will adopt more and more of the simpler fashions of young people, as happened with the trousers and muslins of the early nineteenth century.

Further reading.
Children's Costume in England, 1300–1900, Cunnington and Buck.
The Child in Fashion, Doris Langley Moore.
Modes and Manners from Punch, 1840–1940, Alison Aldburgham.
Handbooks of English Costume (separate small volumes for 5 periods).

Index

The numerals in **bold type** refer to the figure-numbers of the illustrations.